HISTORIC LANDSCAPES
of Florida

Rocco J. Ceo and Joanna Lombard

The Deering Foundation & the University of Miami School of Architecture

Catherine Lynn, editor.
Published by the Deering Foundation and University of Miami School of Architecture.
Book design and typography by Diaz & Cooper Advertising, Inc.
Printed by Dynacolor Graphics, Inc. Printed in the United States of America.

Library of Congess Control Number: 2001130911

ISBN-0-9714066-0-X

ACKNOWLEDGEMENTS

This work is the result of nearly ten years of active study on the part of more than one hundred University of Miami students as well as many people associated with the landscapes, libraries, and archives of Florida. Without thanking all here by name, there are a number of individuals who must be mentioned for their vital assistance. To begin the project, Javier Cenicacelaya, in his capacity as Dean of the School of Architecture at the University of Miami in 1991, noticed the separate work on Florida landscapes that each of the authors was pursuing and suggested the collaboration that led to this publication. Since then, Dean Elizabeth Plater-Zyberk encouraged and supported the research efforts. The University of Miami Max Orovitz Awards in the Arts and Humanities directly supported summer research and the Florida Endowment for the Humanities supported a related study.

Beth Dunlop reviewed the early progress and advised the authors on the potential for an exhibition. Subsequently, Lamar Jernigan Noriega and D'Ann Tollett in the University of Miami's Office of University Advancement prepared a proposal to the Deering Foundation who provided funding for the exhibition and publication. Mr. Charles Seitz of the Deering Foundation offered valuable guidance as the project moved to publication. At the Miami-Dade Park and Recreation Department, Karen Cheney and Howard Gregg helped in the final search for historic materials and loaned drawings for publication. Director Vivian Rodriguez advised on the exhibition and Carlos J. Dunn, Interim Director of the Deering Estate at Cutler, worked closely with the authors on the exhibition while Leslie Williams, Event Coordinator for the Deering Estate at Cutler, assisted Carolyn White of the School of Architecture with planning and scheduling.

Stephan Mecks Jr. and Sr. of Borders Fine Art Framing developed light yet strong frames to permit the work to travel, and assisted with the initial exhibition. Pyramid Photographics and Thompson Photo Lab have been consistent partners in respectively rescuing images and processing thousands of slides. Otmara Diaz-Cooper and Todd Cooper shared the authors' vision for the publication of this work and our enthusiasm for the subject material, as is evidenced in the design of this book.

In addition to the most recent effort in exhibition and publication, during the last ten years many people have assisted the authors and the students with research. Ruthanne Vogel, at the University of Miami's Otto G. Richter Library Archives and Special Collections, and Dawn Hugh of the Research Center at the Historical Museum of Southern Florida were especially helpful in spotting useful materials. The late Mary Phillips' gift of her father's drawings to the Richter Library at the University of Miami, and Faith Reyher Jackson's gift, on behalf of Juliette Phillips Coyle, of Phillips material to the Historical Museum of Southern Florida made possible the research on the William Lyman Phillips landscapes. The photographic collection of the Florida State Archives and the Miami-Dade Public Library also provided valuable material.

Each of the landscapes' current owners or directors, staff members, and volunteers offered specialized guidance and opened archives to the students and authors. In particular, the authors appreciated the extra efforts of Pirjo H. Restina, Bok Tower Gardens; Mary Anna Carroll, Edison House and Gardens; Anne Taylor RSCJ and Suzanne Cooke RSCJ, El Jardin; at Fairchild Tropical Garden, Don Evans, and also the late William Klein and James McLamore who sponsored initial research on the drawings of William Lyman Phillips; Jim Clupper, Branch Manager of the Helen Wadley Branch Library in Islamorada; Jo Bigelow of the Koreshan Unity Board; Robert E. Bowden, Executive Director of Harry P. Leu Gardens; Janet Alford, Executive Director of McKee Botanical Garden; and Doris Littlefield during her term as curator at Vizcaya. David Sacks of Wallace Roberts & Todd shared historic correspondence on McKee; the late Bert Zuckerman of Fairchild Tropical Garden helped uncover images, and Beth Dunlop found several Gleason W. Romer photographs at the Romer Collection of Miami-Dade Public Library. Arva Moore Parks offered important insight on the Deerings and shared Janet Snyder Matthews' invaluable report on Charles Deering's Cutler Estate.

University of Miami faculty members Adib Curé and Carie Penabad with Jorge Planas of Duany Plater-Zyberk & Company generously assisted with drawing revisions at a crucial time. Adjunct Professor Catherine Lynn edited the manuscript, a project that extended over many months and guided the authors from raw materials to readable text. None of this work could have happened without the assistance of Denis Hector, who shared in the journeys to many of these landscapes and helped photograph them, and Maria Nardi, who assisted with initial research on the Koreshan Unity in 1990 and then traveled the state to record historic landscapes. Both Denis and Maria have provided ongoing critical evaluation of the work.

Finally, it should be clear that although there is still much to discuss about these twenty-seven landscapes, there are many more that are not represented here and deserve equal consideration, including Mrs. Potter Palmer's garden in Osprey, the Cummer Garden in Jacksonville or Henry Nehrling's garden in Gotha. Although this collection is neither comprehensive nor conclusive, the authors hope that this initial documentation of many of Florida's most significant historic landscapes will inspire further study as well as greater awareness of an important cultural legacy.

TABLE OF CONTENTS

THE LEGACY OF FLORIDA'S HISTORIC LANDSCAPES

Joanna Lombard

Theodor de Bry, the sixteenth-century publisher, acquired Jacques le Moyne's *Brevis narratio. . .* in 1588. De Bry made new engravings of the Florida paintings and captured the European imagination with his adaptations of the images and narrative.[1] While le Moyne had balanced artistic vision with reportorial accuracy in the paintings of his voyage to Florida with René de Laudonnière in 1564, de Bry offered a more exotic interpretation. He endowed the natives with Olympian proportions and features, familiarized the landscape, and aggrandized the wildlife, initiating what may have been the first published representations of Florida as a fantastic land of wonder.[2]

Using artistic license to move subject matter closer to an ideal is not uncommon, but in Florida, the practice took a less usual twist, and the landscape itself became a canvas upon which more colorful and dramatic features were drawn. The consequences have become significant. Florida's benevolence encouraged the growth not only of exotic plants and animals but also of a human population whose attendant art and commerce has transformed the original landscape, and in particular the coastal wilderness. Much of what remains of mangrove, hammock, pineland, and coastal dunes exists as a result of determined acts of preservation that can be credited to the builders and later, the advocates of Florida's early gardens and parks.

The formidable task of making these gardens, grounds, and parks available to the public has been undertaken by numerous institutions and organizations. Community groups, such as the Indian River Land Trust who restored what is now the McKee Botanical Garden, have rescued important historic landscapes from the most common fate of Floridian land, development as tracts of commercial or residential properties. Once rescued, however, historic landscapes are now preserved and restored using methods that are relatively new to the twenty-first century.

The United States Department of the Interior is still developing standards to assist local organizations with the process. Whatever form those standards take, preservation or restoration must be founded on the solid knowledge of what was intended and realized by the creators of each landscape. That knowledge depends on research. The documentation of the historic landscapes shown here is the result of a range of research that uncovered ample information on some gardens and sparse material on others. In several cases the new drawings are based on measured drawings by the original designers. More often the reconstruction drawings rely on period photographs. For a few landscapes, written texts from the period exist and occasionally the observations of the original designers survive. What these studies uniformly reveal, however, are the rich opportunities these landscapes present for more extensive investigation. Both the primary documents for these places, as well as archaeological studies of the sites are important to an understanding of Florida. These materials guide scholars and enthusiasts in conserving and rebuilding these valuable monuments.

The historic landscapes of Florida offer a window through which one views the meeting of new arrivals and the authentic Florida, where exotic materials were highlighted against a vast native context. In addition to revealing conditions otherwise lost to the present day, the historic landscapes yield lessons about the thoughtful use of plant materials and the wise placement of buildings. The early estates of Miami, for example, were built high upon the ridge of oolitic limestone that still provides protection from storms and floods. These sites commanded expansive views over the mangrove to the bay beyond. Clearings through the mangroves for water landings or vistas were generally judicious and specific. The preservation of wetlands and tree canopy on these sites, as well as the architecture still offer useful models

A number of these gardens and parks were built originally as private estates. Since ancient Rome, estate gardens have been opened to the public on specified occasions and were often represented as important symbols of the community's civic art. Similarly, the expansive Floridian estates, as well as more humble properties, have now become significant civic monuments. These historic landscapes still have the capacity, and in many cases, the size to impart a sense of grandeur far beyond what individual buildings achieve.

The prospect from the plateau of Mountain Lake Sanctuary, or the open ellipse that brilliantly illuminates the fringes of the hammock at McKee Botanical Garden– these are Florida's magnificent salons and halls of public space. Their interweaving of the native and exotic recalls the palaces of the Bourbon kings of France whose walls, stairs, and ornaments come from the native rock of French quarries and whose halls were filled with the art of the world.

At Vizcaya, a visitor to the estate was led through miles of hammock and mangrove that the estate originally encompassed before finally reaching the parterre, a garden room lined with Italian sculpture. Such landscapes remain vigorous, and occasionally, eccentric spaces which still draw people to them and figure prominently in the cultural heritage of the state.

> *"There was the sea and the bay, tranquil and innocent already as blue flowers. There was the rock below, the sun, the fine exuberant air"*
>
> – Marjory Stoneman Douglas

The messages of these gardens are both unique to each setting and common to all. Today, most historic landscapes, even some of best maintained, have been overlaid with new materials and interventions. In some cases, important views within the gardens are affected by the profiles of modern buildings on adjacent and also, distantly related properties. In almost all cases, little remains of the larger context. To reconstruct the historic, designed landscapes, in life and in drawings, is to recreate the experience of the moment when Florida was fresh, its native landscape still intact, its history still connected to a geological time frame.

Marjory Stoneman Douglas, in *The Everglades: River of Grass*, poetically traces Florida's human history back twenty thousand years. Up until the late nineteenth century, urban settlement was limited. Not until Flagler's railroad fully penetrated the state in the opening of the twentieth century did Florida host a significant urban population. The initial encounter of the first wave of pioneers, utopians, adventurers, naturalists, and connoisseurs with Florida's fragile and complex landscape produced important moments in which the confluence of time, culture, and aspiration is revealed. For the next fifty years the changes in Florida's population can be discerned in its gardens and grounds. Reconstructing these landscapes in the new drawings, as well as exhibiting drawings of the period, represents those moments.

Understanding the role of the historic designed landscape, at its inception and in the present can also suggest directions for the future. Offering guidance, Marjory Stoneman Douglas's insightful description of the destruction wrought by the 1926 hurricane is suggestive. After discussing the horror of the storm and the tragic loss of life and property, she noted that:

> *in the ruined city the cheapness, the flimsiness, the real estate shacks, the billboards, the garish swinging signs, the houses badly built, the dizzy ideas, the boom itself, was blown away. What was left were such foundations of buildings or ideas as had been well and truly laid. There was the sea and the bay, tranquil and innocent already as blue flowers. There was the rock below, the sun, the fine exuberant air. And the courage, the fundamental character, of a sobered people.*[3]

The historic landscapes surely were "well and truly laid." The importance of these places today is all the greater for their endurance. When most of these gardens and grounds were originally carved from a native wilderness, the gardens were understood as inspired episodes within a dense context of tropical woods. Now that so little of the original context is left, the native materials that were interwoven within the gardens have become precious remnants of a lost landscape.

The historic gardens are exhilaratingly beautiful. Similar to the realizations of those early citizens in the face of their cataclysmic loss to the hurricane, the view of what remains after the vast storm of Florida's land development is also humbling and sobering. The landscapes presented in these drawings, through their fundamental good sense and clarity of design, can inspire a new relationship in Florida – between its land and its people.

Notes:

1. Stefan Lorant, editor, *The New World: The First Pictures of America made by John White and Jacques le Moyne and engraved by Theodore de Bry with Contemporary Narratives of the Huguenot Settlement in Florida 1562-65 and the Virginia Colony 1585-1590* (New York: Duell, Sloan & Pearce, 1946), 30-31, 280.

2. Lorant 1946, 32, 51-87.

3. Marjory Stoneman Douglas, *The Everglades: River of Grass* (Sarasota: Pineapple Press [1947]1988), 340-341.

REPRESENTATION AS EXPLORATION

Rocco Ceo

Florida's earliest explorers carried not only the rifle and the sword but also the pen and the brush into a field where natural specimens unknown to Europeans abounded. In the middle of the sixteenth century, Jacques le Moyne de Morgues depicted Florida's inhabitants. By detailing their customs, settlement patterns, and the fields they cultivated, and the dense river landscape they inhabited, he preserved for us in visual form, a world that without his work, would have vanished completely. Two centuries later, documenting plants, William Bartram made elegant and careful line drawings that only a trained eye could have produced. Those drawings continue to teach us that looking closely is the fundamental way to avoid running roughshod over a landscape that is both sublime in its grandeur and infinitely fragile in its subtlety. Into the nineteenth century, John James Audubon was still exploring, making hundreds of drawings of the wildlife and the habitats that once blanketed the coasts of Florida from Jacksonville to Key West. His drawings remind us that the lives of creatures and their environments are intimately linked. Within the explorers' tradition, students of Miami's School of Architecture began in 1992 to make drawings that are shown here. Many of the students' works draw upon the botanical studies of Bartram and Audubon. These vignettes frame the maps they accompany and present the viewer with otherwise imperceptible detail, given the map's large scale. As faculty, we have studied with succeeding classes a Florida transformed from the one Europeans found, but in the spirit of the delineators of the past we are seeking the first view and are awestruck by its beauty and wealth of detail.

Making the Drawings

A casual perusal of the drawings on these pages could fail to convey their real value as original contributions to the history of Florida's landscape. These comprehensive, detailed documents take the form of seemingly simple map-like illustrations of parks, gardens and landscapes that have an almost effortless and primitive quality belying the careful research and depth of documentation that necessarily preceded their production. Because in all but Vizcaya, no images comparable to them existed previously, acquiring knowledge of the early appearance of these landscapes to draw them this way required long hours of research, both in the library and in the field. The drawings not only depict the dimensions and spatial qualities of the chosen landscapes, but often also locate and give in detail and overall form the correct species of plants within them. In each case, students worked out an appropriate technique for representing a particular garden or landscape and marked a period of time in that garden's development that might be considered its zenith, isolating for the curious or expectant viewer an ideal image, an image that can be compared and contrasted with the present condition of the place. The drawings that resulted can become both historical documents and tools for reconstruction. The students' approach yielded a direction that can guide constructive groups preserving historical landscapes, or at the very least stand as concrete representations of one ideal giving direction to the development of much needed support for the restoration process at gardens that remain neglected.

Making all these drawings was a Herculean task that took us well outside the confines of standard academic resources and practices. Producing even a single one is a complex and time consuming task; this is why so many gardens have gone undocumented for years and why most guidebooks are illustrated with only a detail from the larger landscape, or a photograph of one area within a much larger construct. Documenting landscapes takes large numbers of researchers and many hours of work. The groups of students who collectively tackled the problem of recording these gardens did so in a spirit of cooperation. Without it, such a cumbersome and time-consuming subject would have defeated the best individuals' efforts.

The large scale of the drawings and their wealth of detail demanded that the students break down the task of documenting their subjects into discrete parts, and set aside personal agendas, so that the drawings could be made in a timely manner. They often divided themselves into teams, first to document different areas of a garden photographically, then with detailed sketches, and finally with measured plans. This method was especially essential in the case of the Ravine Garden in Palatka, where students traveled three hundred miles from Miami and had only limited time to work on site. Here, making the base drawings for a map, student groups had to document bridges, walks, architecture, plant species, and even the section of a ravine in a cold and wet landscape, for it rained continuously the two short days we were there. Understanding other landscapes, such as the Koreshan Unity settlement or The Kampong, required long hours of poring over archival photographs, letters, and planting ledgers to piece together a landscape that had been modified or overgrown or part of which was simply missing from the place we found. Exploring a site also meant a high level of creativity: students had to invent research techniques for ferreting out the essential attributes of the landscape under study. I am proud to say that this kind of commitment to documenting the landscapes was never in short supply over the years.

From this field research, students determined the scale and level of detail that the "underlays", or preliminary drawings, would require. Questions about orientation, scale, borders, amount and style of rendering were discussed collectively through full-scale mock-ups in pencil so that future detail development could remain focused toward the final underlay. These pencil draft underlays would then go through revisions based on composition, content and legibility before being selected for the final underlay. Once the final underlay was produced in pencil, one would then test all decisions affecting the rendering of the final ink drawing. Students would begin the process of the final drawing by producing fully rendered inked test strips of representative sections of the drawing, deciding line weights and density of rendering in order to keep the drawing from becoming too dense when reduced for publication. This ensured that the highest level of craft and draftsmanship would be the rendering standard. Students always kept two audiences in mind: one for the map at full scale, and another that would eventually see the drawing reduced for publication in a book. Such consistency of approach was required from the very beginning of this project recognizing that it would take many years to complete (nine years of drawing), for we wanted the drawings to hang well together, to coexist with a rigor of documentation and clarity of execution that was consistently high. That the students could achieve so high a standard is testament to their collective effort, their ability to visualize the final product and appreciate the value of their endeavor to produce it, and it is a tribute to the school's focus.

Looking at the Maps

Understanding the orientation of the maps is critical to understanding an important point the drawings make. Many of them are oriented to suggest how the gardens were conceived or were entered originally. Many of these gardens pre-date efficient land routes of travel and were usually approached by boat. Therefore their designers located the "front doors" facing rivers, bays, or other watercourses. But now the vehicular entrances are the ones through which we visit these gardens, and since we are essentially entering the sites through their "back doors," it can be difficult to read the original intentions. Many of these drawings reconstruct an original orientation by placing at the bottom of the page the entrance a garden's designer intended, and unfold away from the water's edge, laying back scaled elevations of vegetation and architectural elements alike. This Chinese perspective gives the viewer a preferred view, and recovers the importance of the original entrance. This technique does two important things: first it separates the drawing from the lineage of the aerial photograph that indicates no preferred point of entry, and second it depicts the true species of plants so the viewer can read the landscape without referring to a legend. We found it important to be able to read the gardens so directly and significant to see species differentiated with as much detail as possible, in this subtropical context where the great variety of plant material is something that makes this landscape unique.

The rendering of different species of plant material underscores the commitment to drawing the landscape in detail, not just in overall form, whether in plan, as in Bok Tower, or in elevation, as in the Harry P. Leu Garden. Many landscapes have picturesque paths punctuated by moments of formality, and if abstractly rendered they can look very much alike. But an allée of royal palms is different from an allée of live oaks or of ficus, and the difference in canopy texture and shape creates different qualities of shade. Each landscape's texture and botanical diversity is unique, and omitting the details we have worked to include would have obliterated all sense of the tactile, experiential range of the landscapes depicted here. The primitive quality of the drawings and the inclusion of detail encourage the viewer to distinguish and locate plant materials, to recognize replacement or change through time. The detail refers to the time the gardens were constructed, and in cases where the gardens have been reconstructed, the drawings become especially

valuable documents, since much of those gardens may have been lost to development, neglect, or a changed vision.

Looking at the drawings of le Moyne, Bartram, and Audubon we can wonder about what was here, what is, and what will become of the landscape they explored before us. Like the drawings of their illustrious predecessors, the students' new drawings are interpretations of places that reflect current attitudes, as well as those of the generations of individuals who left their mark on the gardens. Our drawings, with all their detail and representing so many hours of work remain, despite the best efforts, incomplete, for the drawings alone cannot represent the committed individuals who direct and maintain the gardens and the visitors whose donations make possible the very survival of many of these gardens and landscapes. The drawings are also signposts, markers in the constantly changing state that characterizes gardens. The drawings are reminders of the need to make plans for the gardens' continued renewal. We hope that the drawings will be used to build support, and where necessary, to restore what has fallen into disrepair, acting as a foundation for a new preservation effort, to spur more people to assume thoughtful stewardship of the land.

There are many more landscapes to explore, to draw, to preserve, and to restore. We hope these drawings will foster an ongoing program of documentation and reconstruction. It has been part of our mission to create a threshold toward future work, and we hope that these drawings will inspire viewers to visit the places depicted within these pages, and to take up the mission of the gardens' founders and the preservation of those early ideals.

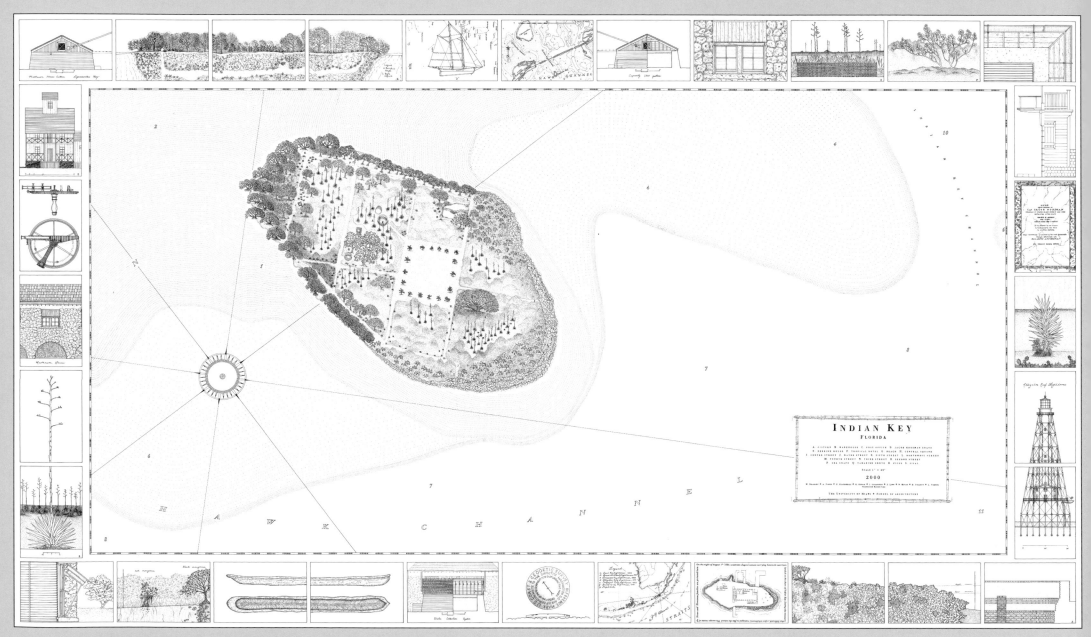

INDIAN KEY
FLORIDA

DRAWING BY: WYNN G. BRADLEY, ANNE FINCH, GINA GIACOBELLI, KEVIN KUNAK, JESS LINN, JOHANNA LUKAUSKIS, NATALIA MIYAR, D'ANN TOLLETT, LUIS TORRES
42" X 71", HORIZONTAL FORMAT, INK ON MYLAR, 2000

Indian Key has, until the present, been one of the oldest continually populated pieces of land in South Florida. From the research of archaeologists we know prehistoric Indian populations inhabited Indian Key. They lived there for thousands of years before the Spaniards sailed down the coast of Florida. After the Spanish exploration, Bahamian wreckers and turtlers occupied Indian Key because it was located conveniently near reefs and fresh water wells on Lower Matecumbe Key.

One of Indian Key's earliest and most colorful figures was Jacob Housman, a wrecker who defected from Key West, purchased the island in 1831, and turned it into his private town, complete with hotel, housing, wharves, post office, and trading store. It was Housman who would be the first white settler to cultivate his land by setting out groves of citrus, and even importing fertile soil for his gardens. It was in part this landscape that must have inspired Dr. Perrine's daughter Hester Perrine when she

Hester Perrine Walker.
Historical Museum of Southern Florida.

first arrived at the tiny island on Christmas morning December 1838:

I cannot forget our delight of first seeing this beautiful little island of only 12 acres. It was truly a "Gem of the Ocean." The trees were many of them covered with morning glories of all colors, while the waving palms, tamarinds, papaws, guavas, seaside grape trees and many others too numerous to mention made it seem to us like fairy land, coming as we did from the midst of snow and ice.[1]

It was probably Charles Howe, an associate to whom Perrine had sent seeds and plants from the Yucatan, who had begun trying out new plants on Indian Key that contributed to Housman's plantings. Therefore, even before arriving at Indian Key, Dr. Henry Perrine, a physician-turned-botanist, would have an impact on its plantings. It was Dr. Perrine who, with the help of a land grant from the U.S. government, pioneered research into tropical plants, leaving his mark on South Florida by providing us with many plants useful to this climate and soil.

Perrine's mission for South Florida can be evidenced in his letter to the House of Representatives on February 3, 1838:

...And I repeat that every future settler in South Florida will be ruined, unless preceded by the associate labor of a company which shall introduce the appropriate plants, and teach the appropriate mode of propagation adapted to the peculiarity of its climate and soil. Hence, also, Texas and Cuba will continue to attract our agricultural emigrants in thousands, and southern Florida will be occupied by a still worse race than the Seminoles.[2]

View of Indian Key in the early 1900s.
Florida State Archives.

This letter to the House of Representatives, was one of many Perrine sent to the U.S. government to convince them that, contrary to reports by the military, South Florida was more than an "impenetrable morass" of mosquitoes and "pestilential swamps." Perrine requested a

Century Plant.
Florida State Archives.

land grant so that he could set up one of the earliest plant introduction and experimental gardens of tropical botany in the country, a request Congress granted in 1838. It was to be the same Seminoles to whom Perrine referred so disparagingly in his letter who would later, during the Seminole Indian War, overrun the small hamlet of Indian Key, take the life of Dr. Perrine and massacre many of the other inhabitants.

Perrine pioneered research into Sisal Hemp or *agave sisalana Perrine* as it is now known, named after its founder. Perrine was interested in establishing sisal hemp for large-scale

> *"It was truly a "Gem of the Ocean." The trees were many of them covered with morning glories of all colors, while the waving palms, tamarinds, papaws, guavas, seaside grape trees and many others too numerous to mention made it seem to us like fairy land…"*
>
> – Hester Perrine Walker

commercial cultivation. Although Perrine failed to achieve this, Florida nurserymen would eventually furnish thousands of seeds and bulbs to other tropical locations such as Java, to create plantations that would keep Mexico from having a complete monopoly on binder twine.

While Perrine is best known for the Sisal plant or agave, he also developed a variety of lemon known as the

Perrine home on Indian Key and escape tunnel to wharf.
Florida State Archives.

Mexican or "Key" lime, later named Perrine, and introduced pineapple and date palms to some of the nearby islands.

Today one can visit the small island of Indian Key, which is now owned by the state of Florida, and find historical markers describing the small wrecking community that once flourished upon its eleven acres. Ruins are to be seen, the foundations of buildings and cisterns, and are punctuated by tall stands of sisal plants, wild coffee, coconuts, and tamarind trees. Along with the recently cut paths and remnants of the town-square laid out in dirt, ruins are all that remain of this early experiment with plant introduction. The tiny island of Indian Key, still accessed only by boat, most conveniently from a nearby marina on Lower Matecumbe Key, stands as a silent reminder of the difficulties and dangers endured by early botanists in introducing tropical plants for cultivation.

–RJC

Notes:

1. Hester Perrine Walker "The Perrines at Indian Key, Florida, 1838-1840," *Tequesta* 7 (1947): 71.

2. Henry Perrine to the "Honorable Members of the Committee on Agriculture of the House of Representatives," February 3, 1838, Library of The Gray Herbarium, Harvard University.

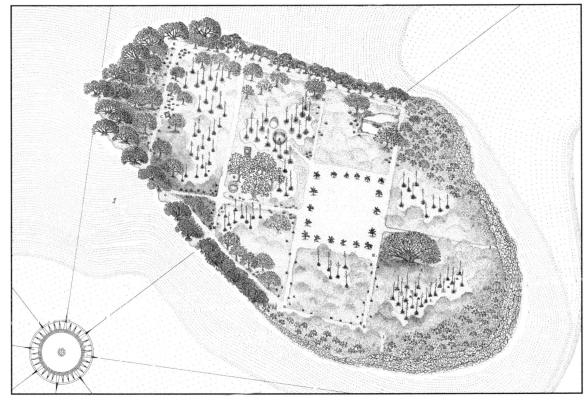

Detail of drawing showing the entire island.

Left to right: Hugh Matheson, R. Cochron, N.L. Britton, J.T. Kennett and unknown gentleman on Indian Key.
Florida State Archives.

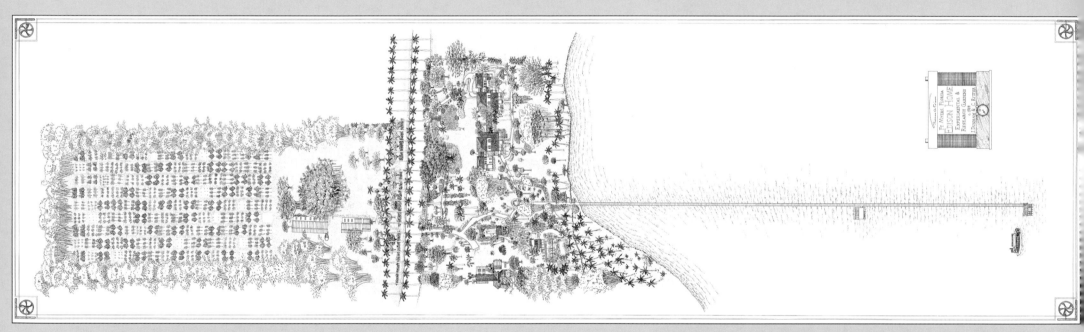

DRAWING BY: VALERY AUGUSTIN, CHRIS RITTER

22" X 73", VERTICAL FORMAT, INK ON MYLAR, 1993

Detail of drawing showing garden divided by McGregor Blvd.

Henry Nehrling, a noted naturalist and author on tropical flora, described in 1929 the tropical estate of the famous inventor of the incandescent light bulb and phonograph:

Though the entire place impresses us as a large forest-like park of a tropical nature, there are many fine groups and open vistas, showing us the placid and glittering waters of the great river. There are many dense rare tropical trees everywhere in the grounds, and there is a wealth of fine dense shrubs everywhere. There is nowhere formality. Everything appears natural. There are three characteristics most evident-individuality, privacy and solitude.[1]

Nehrling's impressions of Thomas Alva Edison's winter home were published by the State Federation of Garden Clubs only two years before the inventor's death. In 1885 Edison had been inspired by the stands of bamboo he found along the shore of the site to embark upon construction of an experimental garden there. That garden would have an impact on many of his early inventions, and on the dissemination and introduction of plants among noted scientists and naturalists throughout South Florida.

Edison, who first came to the site by water, built a long dock to improve access across the shallows of the Caloosahatchee River. His bamboo landing marks the beginning of a collection of experimental and ornamental plants, rich in diversity, and terminates the axial arrangement of the dock. The site stretches deep inland over fourteen acres but is quickly divided across its length into two plots by a boulevard lined with Cuban royal palms. The plot facing the Caloosahatchee River has both buildings and gardens that represent transplantation in very literal ways, for the main house was built off site, far away in Fairfield, Maine, and brought here by water, and many of the plants - in particular the royal palms - arrived as specimens dug in distant forests. Stephan Nye, working in Maine, constructed the house in sections and shipped it to Florida on four schooners. In its design, he and Edison incorporated early notions about living in a tropical climate, aligning windows that encourage cross-ventilation and creating generous porches that protect the house from summer heat and also from driving rains.

Postcard of Edison Home and Garden, bay side
Rollo Cto Collection.

From the house, one has glimpses of the river or can ponder groupings of specimens nearby. These specimens, and others planted within the estate, are part of one of the oldest and most significant experimental industrial botanical gardens in the United States. The experimental garden surely has a long history, but few before

Postcard showing home viewed from the Caloosahatchee River.
Rocco Ceo Collection.

reinforcing with Portland cement in the concrete he made for his own swimming pool.

During the First World War, Edison focused on finding rubber, which was strategically necessary and had become scarce. This work put Edison in contact with many naturalists, plant explorers, and industrialists. Among them

content necessary for manufacturing rubber. Harvey Firestone was sent samples of it to consider what could be done if goldenrod were grown in large quantities. Although it never went into large-scale production, Edison did use it to make a set of tires for his own Model T that is currently on exhibition at the museum on the site.

"There are many dense rare tropical trees everywhere in the grounds, and there is a wealth of fine dense shrubs everywhere. There is nowhere formality. Everything appears natural."

– Dr. Henry Nehrling

this one focused on industrial applications. Most early experimental gardens were for medicinal or agricultural purposes. Edison's great interest in the by-products of tropical plants spurred him to develop a garden that served his experiments at the same time it simply pleased him with the beauty of its tropical flowers. Among the specimens that proved most significant for his work was bamboo. Edison found that the tough fibers were both workable and efficient. When they were carbonized, they became durable filaments capable of long service in his first electric light bulbs. The inventor also tested bamboo as an inexpensive and readily available reinforcement for concrete. He tried out bamboo

Postcard, Rocco Ceo Collection.

were Harvey Firestone, the industrial giant who manufactured tires, and David Fairchild, the plant explorer and botanist who so significantly shaped the Florida landscape. This sequence of events indicates the importance of botanical research, not only to South Florida but also to the rest of the country.

Edison also considered the possibility that rubber might be extracted from the poisonous plant oleander, but he eventually settled on goldenrod because he found that it had a milky sap with the high latex

It should also be noted that Edison's garden was perhaps the earliest to be artificially lighted by electricity, and that in 1885 he designed a system of underground electric lines so that

View from porch towards bay.
Photograph by R. Ceo.

Postcard depicting Memory Garden.
Rocco Ceo Collection.

he could remove unsightly wires from view and give his plants unencumbered growing room. It became a place to be seen in the evening. With a flip of the switch, Edison could now selectively accent garden features. And his switches were waterproof and vapor-proof.

This garden's significance lies not only in its role as a precursor, setting an example for gardens of the modern era in which experiments applicable to industry were conducted, but also in the range of species Edison collected for it. Edison's garden is a careful blend of plants chosen for scientific study as well as for the pleasure and beauty associated with a private retreat.

Many gardens in Florida followed Edison's lead, and let their botanical interests determine the ways they laid out their plots. And many, like Edison, treat plants as accents, perhaps where the perfume might be enjoyed through a bedroom window or a collection of plants might add accents of color when viewed from a porch.

Edison's garden, and many that have been inspired by it, are practical places where we are reminded that many of the things we enjoy in the modern world, including some of the most artificial conveniences, have natural origins.

–RJC

Notes:

1. Dr. Henry Nehrling et al., *My Garden in Florida*, vol.1 (Estero: Koreshan Unity Press, 1944), 199-200.

Entrance from bay.
Photograph by R. Ceo.

DRAWING BY: CHRIS JACKSON
24" X 36", HORIZONTAL FORMAT, INK ON MYLAR, 1992

The Barnacle from the edge of Biscayne Bay.
Photograph by R. Ceo.

In all of South Florida there is no structure that, with its landscape, represents early attempts to live in a tropical landscape better than the Barnacle. In 1891 Ralph Middleton Munroe built the house on a five-acre lot, high on an oolitic limestone ridge overlooking Biscayne Bay. The house is an excellent example of local vernacular architecture with its deep porches, hipped roof, and wood-frame construction. It is oriented toward the bay, the primary point of entry. Munroe, in facing his house away from the land, demonstrates that for him the overland route was a last resort, if not an impossible way to travel, given the density of a landscape through which roads and bridges had not yet penetrated.

Munroe made many photographs in and around Biscayne Bay. He recorded the faces of Mariah Brown, Kirk Munroe and Chief Tigertail, as well as those of friends and neighbors, including the Peacocks, the McFarlanes, and the Beasleys. In dozens of photographs that record visitors to his house, the pioneers' pride in having found a new paradise is revealed. The portraits of friends inevitably feature a palm, citrus, or papaya tree as the backdrop suggesting the travelers' engagement with the tropical and the exotic. It is easy to forget how strange the flora must have

seemed to the northern visitor, unfamiliar with the strangler fig, the papaya, and even the coconut palm.

Munroe's interest and experience designing and building shallow draft boats directed his

Hammock with early visitors.
Archives and Special Collections, Otto G. Richter Library
University of Miami

lens to document in an encyclopedic manner the great numbers of sailing vessels on the bay. His photographs show us how important access to the water was for work and pleasure, and they make it clear that the bay was Coconut Grove's most important public space, a great piazza of water. From the bay, one had a magnificent view of the landscape, which was difficult to see from within. Because it was hard to clear the dense, heavy wood of hammock land, early builders perched their houses at the top of the oolitic limestone ridge on the edge of the hammock, just above the rising water, removing only enough of the hammock to create a site for building. Mangroves, blocking routes to the water, were

Dock into bay.
Photograph by R. Ceo.

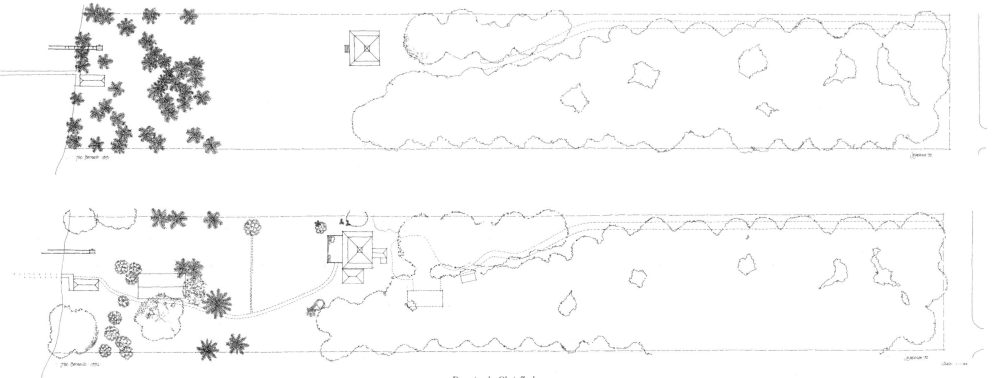

Drawing by Chris Jackson

removed to provide access to the bay as well as views and breezes to the house.

Cleared land in front of the houses was then planted with palms and fruit trees. Occasionally, exotic flowering trees were added, probably because the early black Bahamian settlers in the area, who were familiar with tropical landscapes, shared their knowledge. The more open landscape that settlers began to create in the late 1880s contrasted sharply with the hammock.

Lurking just beyond the ridge, the hammock was a dark tangle of unfamiliar plants, a labyrinthine place capable of creating confusion and disorientation. The impression the hammock made on a frequent visitor to the Barnacle, Kirk Munroe, is reflected in one of the many novels he wrote for boys. The author, who was not related to the Barnacle's owner, set fictive stories in real places. In his story of a homestead in the Everglades called "Big Cypress" there is a moment in which the strange

landscape figures largely. Monroe writes of a Mr. Lawton, who disappearing into the hammock "one evening he failed to come home, nor was any trace of him to be found afterwards."[1]

The Barnacle circa 1894.

Current house as seen from below bluff.
Photograph by R. Ceo.

In the real life of Ralph Munroe, a day's outing from the Barnacle typically meant difficulty traveling, given the sharp, oolitic rock on the ground and the potential to lose himself hopelessly in a tangle that might afford unobstructed views only if he kept to well defined paths. Ralph Munroe wrote a book in 1930 in which he described the difficulty of

Landscape between house and bay.
Archives and Special Collections, Otto G. Richter Library, University of Miami.

reaching a stand of royal palms in this landscape during the 1880s:

> *A pleasant incident of this winter was the visit of the late Charles Sargent, the well-known botanist, with Mrs. Sargent and Mr. Codman, on the Lighthouse tender laurel. In their company I spent a pleasant week, and acquired more technical knowledge of the country's floral beauties than I had dreamed of. Among other things I showed them a Royal Palm Grove in the mangrove swamp south of Little River, which delighted Sargent extremely, though the labor of reaching it was too much for the rest of the party.*[2]

Visiting the Barnacle today conveys some sense of this original condition because a reserve of hammock buffers the site from the intrusive development along parts of the Barnacle's perimeter. This site, so important to this early history of homesteading and life on the bay, stands alone today, no longer within a wilderness, but as an island of hammock and garden amidst the commerce of the surrounding community.

–RJC

Royal palm near New River, R. Munroe.
Archives and Special Collections, Otto G. Richter Library, University of Miami.

Notes:

1. Kirk Munroe, *Big Cypress. The Story of an Everglade Homestead* (Boston: W. A. Wilde & Co., 1894), 7.

2. Ralph Middleton Munroe, *The Commodore's Story* (Ives Washburn, 1930), 146.

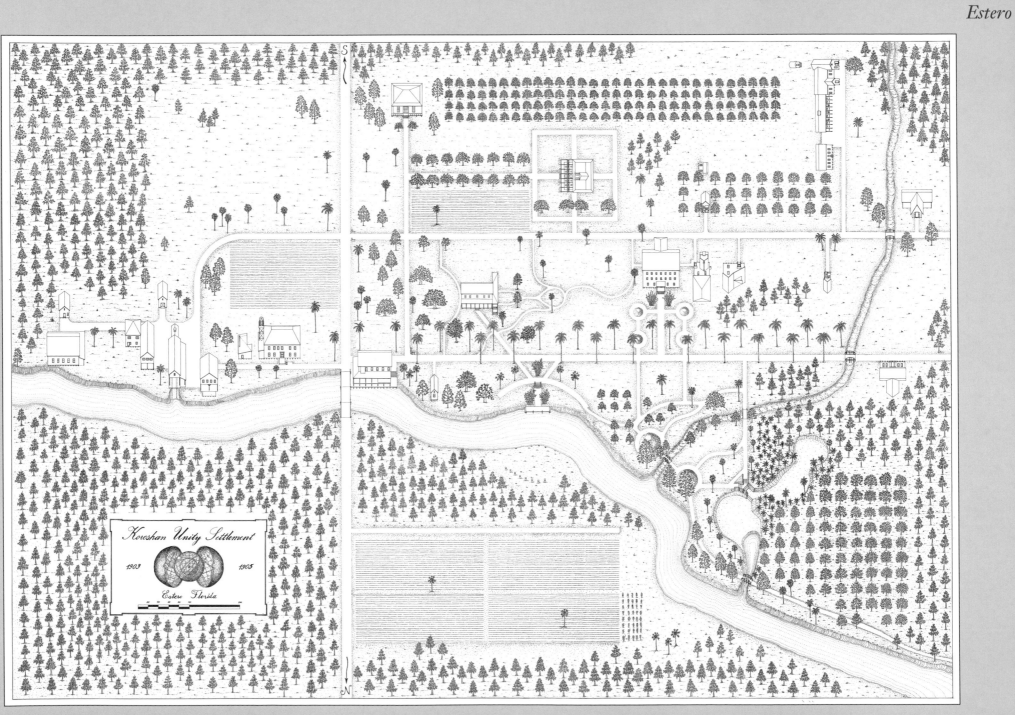

Koreshan Unity Settlement

1903   1905

Estero Florida

Drawing by: Adib Cure, Chris Goertz
36" x 48½", horizontal format, ink on mylar, 1993

D r. Cyrus Teed founded "The Koreshan Unity," in Chicago in 1888.[1] The Koreshans were utopians who believed in a complete religious, scientific, and social system – the "Koreshan Universology." Florence Fritz describes Teed's association with Gustave Damkohler, a septuagenarian who joined the Koreshans in 1894 and gave the Unity three hundred acres for a "Settlement" in Estero, Florida. A number of Koreshan communities had moved from around the country to Chicago just before the community moved to Florida.[2] In addition to the land provided by Damkohler, Teed added another thousand acres where the Unity would practice the doctrines of Koreshanity and from which it could spread its theories and teachings until the whole world was converted.[3]

The land that was to become the New Jerusalem was still a wilderness in 1894. Upon their arrival, the two hundred settlers who accompanied Teed turned to the nearby cypress swamps for logs and began to build.[4] The early Koreshans established an area they called "The Home Grounds," designed to become the center of a new city. Most of the buildings that would provide for immediate physical comfort and basic

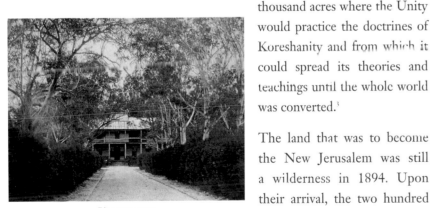

Planetary court.
Collection Koreshan Unity Alliance.

needs were sited in the Home Grounds, awaiting the time when the Unity would construct the New Jerusalem.[5]

The site for the New Jerusalem was determined to be the center of the world, recalling medieval depictions of the original Jerusalem as the navel of the world. Centrality is a theme that recurs throughout the Koreshans' designs for their buildings, landscape, and city plan, as well as in descriptions of the site, bounded by Estero Bay and the Gulf of Mexico, that:

is on the natural line of commerce from North to South America, and transversely east and west from Asia, across Nicaragua, the Gulf of Mexico, through a ship canal across the peninsula of Florida, to New York and across the Atlantic ocean.[6]

Their project for New Jerusalem, a nine-square grid of six square miles, included a system of formal gardens laid out in geometric patterns, with buildings in various architectural styles.[7] The Koreshan journal, the *Flaming Sword*, in October of 1896 envisioned a city with advanced technological improvements that would be sensitive to the environment and corrective of many of the ills of modern urban life. It was to be a city of:

such proportions of magnitude and progress in its development as to become permanent in its architectural creation, the underground or

basement will be an excavation walled in to complete a system of intercommunication for cables, wires and perpetually moving platforms for the transportation of debris and offal, which will be deodorized with earth and chemicals and conveyed to a spot 40 or more miles from the city where it will be reduced to fertilizer and returned to the soil. There will be no dumping of the public waste into the rivers, bays, and gulfs. . .There will be no telegraphic or telephonic wires overhead to mar the beauty of the city. . .The various kinds of traffic, travel, and transportation will be arranged on planes of different elevations, so as to provide against the commotion, disorder, inconvenience, and danger that now characterize all large cities.[8]

Koreshan religion and philosophy set the ideas for the layout of the master plan. Two diagonal main streets that ran north-south and east-west divided the grid of thirty-six squares. A temple dominates, placed at the intersection of the two diagonals. Sixteen thousand feet in diameter, the temple would be surrounded by a "crystal sea," three hundred feet wide, and by "eight parks in the shape of a parabola adjusted to an octagonal street."[9] The park system contained almost all other buildings and is described as filled with fruit and nut trees and with other plants chosen from biblical descriptions of Eden.[10]

Three geometric elements - the arc, chord, and radius resound through the landscape. Koreshan belief in the cellular nature of the universe is tangibly represented in the layout of the city by concentric rings that encircle the center and by the joining of circles and squares which occurs at the intersections of the grid. These geometric relationships parallel the growth of the settlement, which reflects cellular growth, the Koreshan model of the universe.

Mound garden.
Photograph by R. Ceo.

As the intersections of the orthogonal lines are marked with circles, the intersection of the circle with the square forms an octagon, a form that art historian John Onians traces to St. Ambrose's "inscription for a baptistry drawing attention to the meaning of its eight corners, eight being associated with the eighth day of the new Creation and Christ's Resurrection on the eighth day of the Passion."[11] The continuous circles in the Koreshan plan refer to a common understanding within the community that eschewed private ownership and shared all resources. The placement of the temple within the central circle confirms the central role of faith as the paradigm for the physical landscape.

Within the Home Grounds, the starting point of the New Jerusalem, the largest buildings included a three-story structure with a dining hall and dormitory rooms, a Planetary Court, and a residence for the Unity's women leaders, as well as smaller separate dorms for men and for women,

a house for Dr. Teed and a school. In accordance with the community's goal of self-sustenance, a print shop and a bakery were constructed early on as well as industrial buildings with adjoining dorms for the men who worked in them. A store and a steam laundry took care of other needs. Still other buildings of the Home Grounds included a boat house and a green house.

All of these structures were located within the park system, while barns for livestock, dairy and other necessary buildings were placed beyond the limits of the park.[12] Current speculation, based upon Moses Weaver's painting of the 1902 master plan, focuses on the possibility that the Koreshans intended eventually to use stone on all buildings located in the parks.[13] The founder's house gives some evidence that it underwent such a process of transformation from wood to stone.

A plan of the settlement in the Weaver painting illustrates the Home Grounds, also known as the Koreshan Tropical Botanical Gardens.[14] While much of the New Jerusalem remained a visionary scheme, the Home Grounds were built and served the community which ranged from two hundred at its peak in 1908,

Fountain with urn.
Collection Koreshan Unity Alliance.

to a solitary few fifty years later. At the outset, however, the gardens of the Home Grounds were carved from the mangrove and from stands of pine trees,

saw palmetto trees, and scrub oaks. Practical items, including patches of sweet potatoes, yams, cabbages, beets, turnips, beans, peas, tomatoes, eggplants, melons, onions, and Irish potatoes, were grown to support the community.[15] Orchards were another resource and included two types: some with a single type of fruit tree such as orange or grapefruit, and others with a wide variety that may have included combinations of avocado, lemon, lime, mango, tamarind, fig, olive, banana, guava, date, and sugar apple trees or cocoanut palms as well as trees that bore nuts.[16]

Four mounds facing the gardens were built up of soil to rise about three feet above the ground with diameters of about ten feet. Period photographs show the mounds covered with crushed shell and grass forming concentric rings. These formations of earth were crisp in definition and actually composed of what appear to be three distinct levels. Mrs. Jo Bigelow, President of the Koreshan Unity Foundation in 1990, recounted the general association of Dr. Teed with the sun, woman with the moon, and children with the stars.[17] The mounds may have figured in the enactment of that allegory. The four mounds also may have represented the four poles — light, dark, morning and evening — which in the Koreshan cosmology accounted for the origin of the stars and planets. The number four also makes reference to the four winds of heaven, the four foundations of earth, and the four seasons, all of which figure in Koreshan explanations of Cellular Cosmogony.[18]

The settlers also developed gardens to give aesthetic pleasure, or perhaps to reference special spiritual connotations, but in any case they were not strictly useful gardens that yielded produce. The sunken gardens and a "bamboo landing" are examples of such designed landscapes. In a recent report on the Koreshan Unity Settlement written for the State of Florida, G.M. Herbert and I.S.K.

Bamboo landing.
Collection Koreshan Unity Alliance.

Reeves described several of the gardens in detail, basing their description on analysis of photographs, oral interviews, and archival research. They determined that the sunken gardens were located "on the south bank at a bend in the river, just west of the drainage canal, and were constructed under the direction of Dr. Teed around 1904-5." The gardens:

> *consisted of a series of terraces, mounds and steps leading down to a recessed area and the terraces were built up into triangular mounds which were covered with grasses from Cuba. The steps leading down into the gardens were formed with wood headers and packed with crushed shell as were the walks leading to it. There were banana trees adjacent to this area and other fruit trees. . . located just to the west of the gardens.*[19]

A riverside landing planted with bamboo was important both aesthetically and functionally. Herbert and Reeves believed the landing was the setting "for concerts by the Koreshan Unity band until the construction of the Art Hall about 1905. . .It was also used as a stage for a water pageant presented at the celebration of the Solar Festival."[20] Shell paths throughout the settlement were both functional and aesthetically pleasing. The crushed shells made walking considerably easier than did soft sand or dirt, and on the shells, footsteps can be easily heard. The patterns of the silvery paths glowing in the reflected moonlight make a nighttime garden composition dynamic with reflected light, both useful and beautiful.

The gardens also used exotic material, including the monkey puzzle tree, the eucalyptus, and the bamboo to mark points of entry to the community. Exotic trees planted along the Estero River stood out against the background of the indigenous landscape to indicate the boundaries of the community. Within the gardens, footbridges were built of intricately detailed wood panels and masonry piers. The piecework of the panels reflects the Koreshans' general preoccupation with geometric divisions and offers a sharp-edged counterpoint to the tropical foliage. The community's concrete works, in collaboration with its sculpture department, produced the patterned concrete bridges. Community members "busied" themselves

"making medallions, vases, urns, plaques, figure heads and all manner of ornamentation."[21]

The Koreshan Unity Settlement represented one early group's vision of the New Jerusalem as an earthly paradise. The philosophical, religious, and social beliefs of the community shaped the master plan and the gardens. Dr. Teed, in his role as the sun, emphasized his central position figurally and physically. He occupied the house in the center of the Home Grounds and his death in 1908 had a profound impact upon the community.[22] Many settlers lost faith, abandoning the building of the New Jerusalem, and increasingly fewer settlers remained in the

Founder's House.
Photograph by R. Ceo.

community. In 1961, Hedwig Michel, who had joined the community in 1940, and the Koreshan Unity Board gave the 300-acre site to the State of Florida Department of Natural Resources which maintains the site as a state park. In 1990, The Koreshan Unity Alliance, a state charter Citizens Support Organization for the Koreshan State Historic Site, with assistance from the Florida Department of State's Division of Historical Resources, engaged Abell Garcia Architects to develop a restoration master plan for the 10 acres of the original Home Grounds.[23] Restoration work was completed on Damkohler's cottage, the Founders Hall and some of the garden paths. The Founders Hall restoration won an award for outstanding achievement in 1993 from the Florida Trust for Historic Preservation. The Planetary Court, Art Hall and the body of the gardens await restoration funding.

Lunar Festival.
Collection Koreshan Unity Alliance.

Since the sixteenth century, people have come to Florida with the hope of finding a fortune, or making one quickly. In the modern popular imagination, especially since the land boom of the 1920s, Florida has become synonymous with profiteering land development. Members of the Koreshan Unity Settlement arrived before the boom and for quite different reasons. Land speculation was not their motive. These pioneers settled the land to live a faith and in doing so built a community that gave tangible form to their

beliefs. Even though the New Jerusalem remained a vision, the Home Grounds represent the beginning of the utopia they hoped to build.

–JL

Notes:

1. Elliot J. Mackle, Jr., "The Koreshan Unity in Florida 1894-1910" (Master's Thesis, University of Miami, 1971), 17-18.

2. Gerard Wertkin, "Solar Festival Celebrates 145th Anniversary," *The American Eagle* Vol.65 No. 194 (October 1984): 1.

3. Florence Fritz, *Unknown Florida* (Coral Gables: University of Miami Press 1963), 102-3.

4. Cathy Hollopeter, Bonita Banner, "Koreshan Solar Festival commemorates founder's birth," *The American Eagle* Vol. 66 No. 195 (June 1985): 1.

5. Mackle, 1971, 11-25.

6. *Flaming Sword* Vol. X, No. 10, (October 1896): 226.

7. Joseph Lloyd, "Koreshan Unity Plant Nursery and Botanical Gardens." *The American Eagle* Vol. 68, No. 199 (April 1987): 8.

8. *Flaming Sword* Vol. X, No. 10, (October 1896): 226.

9. *Flaming Sword* Vol. X, No. 10, (October 1896): 226.

10. *Flaming Sword* 10 1896, 10; Genesis 1:11-31.

11. John Onians, *Bearers of Meaning: The Classical Orders in Antiquity, the Middle Ages, and the Renaissance* (Princeton: Princeton University Press, 1989), 69.

12. Mackle, 1971, 68-71.

13. Maria Turney, "Koreshan Unity Settlement," http://getp.freac.fsu.edu/fga/places/koreshan.htm

14. Lloyd, 1987, 8.

15. *Flaming Sword* 9 (1896), 203.

16. *Flaming Sword* 9 (1895), 204; (1906), 6; Koreshan Unity 1907, 50.

17. Interview, Mrs. Jo Bigelow, August 16, 1990.

18. Koresh [Cyrus R. Teed], *The Cellular Cosmogony: The Earth a Concave Sphere*, (1898, reprint, Estero: The Koreshan Unity, (1922) 1983), 88.

19. G.M Herbert and I.S.K. Reeves, "Koreshan Unity Settlement 1894 - 1977," Restoration Study for the Department of Natural Resources (Division of Recreation and Parks, State of Florida, 1977), 125-6.

20. Herbert and Reeves 1977,124.

21. Herbert and Reeves, 1977, 129.

22. Gerard Wertkin, "Solar Festival Celebrates 145th Anniversary." *The American Eagle* Vol.65 No. 194 (October 1984): 1.

23. "Koreshan Unity Alliance Members to Lobby State Legislators for Founder's House," and "The Koreshan Unity Alliance Seeks New Members," *The American Eagle* Vol.74 No. 205 (April 1990): 3.

THE DEERING ESTATES IN FLORIDA

Joanna Lombard

Until the twentieth century, Florida's isolation and unrest limited its development. Then in 1912 Henry Flagler's railroad reached Key West and three years later more than 1,000 Miamians welcomed Carl Fisher and his Dixie Highway Pathfinders to the end of the first road trip on the fully completed Dixie Highway into Miami. Fisher and his compatriots had driven for sixteen days from Chicago, where Fisher had made his fortune developing and marketing Prest-O-Lite, the first practical automobile headlight that made night travel possible.[1]

Now that Florida was thoroughly connected to the rest of the U.S., Carl Fisher had arrived to take advantage of booming land sales. With John Collins and the Lummus brothers, Fisher helped transform a barrier island into Miami Beach, a tropical paradise for the upper middle class, complete with exotic plants, animals and Florida's first bathing beauties. Florida's own native plants, animals, and perhaps its humans also, lacked the zesty intensity of the more fantastic specimens Fisher introduced to Miami Beach. The neon pink of the flamingo was much more exciting than the pale white ibis, or even the subtle coloration of the blue heron. The beach itself was redesigned: a slim fringe at the edge of a mangrove became a vast, sandy promenade.

At the same time, James and Charles Deering were pursuing an alternative vision that valued and conserved the native landscape. James Deering acquired the land that would become Vizcaya on New Year's Eve, 1912. Charles Deering began his estate in Buena Vista at the opening of the century, and assembled the first of his Cutler property in 1913. The family patriarch, William Deering, who had spent winters in the Miami area since the closing years of the nineteenth century, had bought a "small agricultural equipment plant" in 1870.[2] By the time William Deering & Company had become the Deering Manufacturing Company in 1883, both brothers had joined the business, James in 1879 and Charles in 1881.[3] The Deerings merged the company in 1890 with the family firm founded by Cyrus McCormick, their leading competitor. In 1902 J.P. Morgan financed the larger merger of the combined firm with several smaller manufacturers to form The International Harvester Company. Charles was chairman of the board for eight years, and James was a vice-president for eighteen years, as well as a life-long member of the board.[4]

James Deering was known for his interest in the mechanics of the farm equipment the company produced and related inventions; Charles Deering was considered the business strategist. James Deering kept a home in Neuilly, outside Paris, and was made a chevalier of the Legion of Honor and *Merite Agricol* of France for his contribution to French agriculture.[5] In an elegiac biography, Walter Dill Scott and Robert Harshee credit Charles with the acquisition of raw material used in manufacturing. To this end, the company acquired "iron mines, coalfields, furnaces and timberlands."[6] Charles Deering's earlier experience in the U.S. Navy, as well as company travel for both brothers provided each with access to the world's art and furnishings, some of which would find a home in their estates.

Toward the end of William Deering's life, he moved south from St. Augustine, Florida, to Miami, where he died in December of 1913. Charles Deering had been wintering at the estate he had established in Buena Vista, north of Miami, but after his father's death, he began to accumulate land parcels for the Cutler property, about twenty miles south of Miami on the shore of Biscayne Bay. About the same time, James Deering had initiated work at Vizcaya, in Coconut Grove, just south of downtown Miami.

Among the few archival remains of Buena Vista are watercolors of a villa and gate house, designed by Clinton Mackenzie, a New York architect, that depict a courtyard villa and a slightly more rustic gatehouse.[7] Mackenzie had designed manufacturing towns and was known in Florida as the architect hired by developers Glenn Curtiss and James Bright to design Arabian Nights style buildings in the new town of Opa-locka just north of Miami.[8] Mackenzie's portfolio furnishes some of the few surviving images of Buena Vista, which is also represented in the photographs of John Kunkel Small.[9]

David Fairchild in his memoir of 1938, *The World Was My Garden*, described Charles Deering's efforts to begin at Buena Vista "what he thought would some day be an Arboretum."[10] Eleanor Bisbee, writing for the *Miami Daily Metropolis* in 1922, mentioned the cactus plantation that

View of proposed Buena Vista Court Garden.
Watercolor, Clinton Mackenzie Architect.
Historical Museum of Southern Florida.

View of Buena Vista photographed by John Kunkel Small.
Historical Museum of Southern Florida.

Charles Deering and John Kunkel Small had launched on the estate.[11] And twenty-five of Buena Vista's 212 acres were loaned to the United States Department of Agriculture for its Seed and Plant Introduction Section, headed by David Fairchild and Edward Simmonds. The estate included two miles of canals with mangroves to provide for an animal habitat. In addition to crocodiles and alligators, Deering imported monkeys and exotic birds. Eventually the zoo was eliminated and the property was sold in the twenties. Janet Snyder Matthews, in a historical documentation report "The Charles Deering Estate at Cutler," suggests that the trouble and cost of the vast aviary at Buena Vista may have inspired Deering later to establish his Cutler estate as a bird habitat distinctly without cages.[12]

Buena Vista is interesting as a precursor of Vizcaya. The drawings for the villa at Buena Vista as a courtyard building closely surrounded by geometric gardens with a cultivated landscape and wilderness beyond reveal a design strategy similar to that which F. Burrall Hoffman Jr. would utilize later at Vizcaya. Contrasting with elaboration of the courtyard villa at Buena Vista is the simplicity of the subsequent Charles Deering house at Cutler, and its inversion of the relationships of interior and exterior space found in Mackenzie's plans for Buena Vista. Where Mackenzie had surrounded an open courtyard with rooms, Phineas Paist, the architect at Cutler, wrapped open porches around the major rooms.

Buena Vista also sustains the historian's interest because the people associated with it were important to South Florida. David Fairchild, the renowned plant explorer, was active at Buena Vista. Later, in 1938, Fairchild recalled that "to add to the galaxy of interesting plant enthusiasts, Mr. [Charles] Deering had brought from Chicago the great landscape gardener O.C. Simonds to layout his estate" at Buena Vista.[13] *The Miami Herald* in August of 1924 credited Frank Button, a former associate of O.C. Simonds, with the design of "the Charles Deering Estate at Buena Vista and his home at Cutler."[14] At that time, Button was the landscape architect for George Merrick's new town of Coral Gables, then in its early stages

of development. Button's work in Coral Gables departed from current procedures for developing landscape in many new towns. Rather than clearing the site, Button preserved existing conditions, both the native pineland and the citrus groves that had been planted around the turn of the century by the Merrick family. Button wanted to create for Coral Gables, streets that would be "veritable bowers laden with delectable fruit."[15] In contrast to the garden city movement's incorporation of individual and collective gardens within a ring of green around the city center, the entire city of Coral Gables was designed by Button as a garden with elaborate vistas, garden rooms, and even urban-scale follies.

Button's urban work conforms to principles Simonds published in 1920 in his book *Landscape Gardening*, part of Liberty Hyde Bailey's *Rural Science* series. Simonds established his aim as the beautification of America. The first principle he defined was unity, which in landscape gardening meant creating a "predominating view."[16] Simonds added other compositional principles including balance, harmony, contrast, variety, and, when seeking repose, repetition.[17] The person expected to accomplish these goals was the landscape-gardener who "may be thought of as trying to produce a Garden of Eden, a garden which is purely imaginary but is thought of as the work of a Power greater than man and more beautiful than anything the present generation has seen."[18]

Landscape in Buena Vista.
Photograph by John Kunkel Small. Historical Museum of Southern Florida.

The design of Buena Vista may relate to the landscape of Coral Gables. Certainly the mingling of native and exotic material that is visible in the surviving photographs of this long demolished estate must have held important lessons for Frank Button that he was able to apply later in Coral Gables. Until more material on Buena Vista comes to light, the property remains enigmatic, although its effect on others is tangible.

David Fairchild wrote in 1938 about an afternoon many years earlier that he spent with the Deerings when Charles Deering was still located in Buena Vista and James Deering's architects were designing Vizcaya. He recalled Charles Deering's Buena Vista Estate "where beautiful canals wound through the mangrove forest and beneath overarching coconut palms," noting that it "contained a collection of succulents planted by Doctor John K. Small and an arboretum of rare trees, many supplied by our Office, aviaries of egrets and cranes, and even an island with monkeys on it." Fairchild lamented its loss:

> *It all disappeared overnight in the boom of 1925 and 1926. Even the magnificent* Ficus nitida *tree, the wonder of the Miami region, was torn to pieces and dragged out by tractors as the entire place was turned into a ghastly waste of suburban lots which to this day have not been sold. This wrecked land is a tragic memorial of those crazy, mad days in which the trees of the "hammocks" went down, destroyed by an army of road builders, carpenters, and cement mixers.*

And Fairchild reflected "how differently the dreams of these two wealthy men materialized." While Charles Deering's Buena Vista had vanished,

> *'Vizcaya,' James Deering's dream, remains a place of strange, tropical beauty. One winter it was open to the public and thousands of visitors who had never seen a palace or European garden could wander there and imagine they were visiting some Italian Renaissance villa set on the shore of an aquamarine bay where palms and tropical trees grow instead of columnar Italian cypresses.*

Fairchild recalled that on the same afternoon:

> *Professor [Charles Sprague] Sargent arrived on what proved to be his last trip to Florida. Together we visited the Cutler Hammock, then the finest hammock land remaining in this region. Sargent remarked that this hammock was the best site for an arboretum that he knew of in Southern Florida.*[19]

Professor Sargent was prescient in his view that the Cutler region held opportunity. What Fairchild could not know in 1938 was the extent to which Charles Deering's rescue of the land that made up his Cutler Estate would become significant, although Fairchild was able to see the effect of Vizcaya on the public. The interests of the Deerings in the native landscape provided for future generations two important preserves that interweave natives and exotics in a harmonious whole and offer a rare view of what the region's earliest settlers discovered and made new.

–JL

Notes:

1. Arva Moore Parks and Gregory W. Bush, *Miami The American Crossroad A Centennial Journey 1896-1990* (Needham Heights, MA: Prentice Hall), 31-2.

2. Janet Snyder Matthews, Historic Documentation: *The Charles Deering Estate at Cutler* (Metro Dade County Park and Recreation Department, 1992), 50.

3. Matthews, 1992, 53.

4. Matthews, 1992, 55.

5. James T. Maher, *The Twilight of Splendor: Chronicles of the Age of American Places* (New York: Little Brown, 1975), 162.

6. Matthews, 1992, 55.

7. Charles Deering Collection, Historical Museum of Southern Florida.

8. Catherine Lynn, "Dream and Substance: Araby and the Planning of Opa-locka," Florida Theme Issue: *The Journal of the Decorative and Propaganda Arts 1875-1945* 23 (1998): 166.

9. J.K. Small Collection, Florida Department of State, Division of Library and Information Services, Bureau of Archives and Records Management, online at: http://www.dos.state.fl.us/fpc

10. David Fairchild, *The World Grows Round My Door* (New York: Charles Scribner's Sons), 1947, (56).

11. Eleanor Bisbee, "It is Extremely Simple to Plant Cactus and the Deering Plantation Gives Proof that Western Varieties Will Grow Here," *The Miami Daily Metropolis*, Monday September 25, 1922.

12. Matthews, 1992, 86.

13. Fairchild, 1947, 57.

14. "An Artist of the Out-of-Doors Made Coral Gables a City of Beauty Spots," *The Herald*, Miami, Florida, 17 August 1924.

15. Frank Button, "The Suburb Beautiful," *Coral Gables, Miami's Master Suburb* (1921), 14.

16. O.C. Simonds, *Landscape Gardening* (New York: The Macmillan Company, 1920, reprint edition, Amherst: University of Massachusetts Press in association with the Library of American Landscape History, 2000), 8.

17. Simonds, [1920] 2000, 13.

18. Simonds, [1920] 2000, 18.

19. David Fairchild, *The World Was My Garden* (1938 Reprint, Miami: Banyan Books Inc., for Fairchild Tropical Garden, 1982), 419.

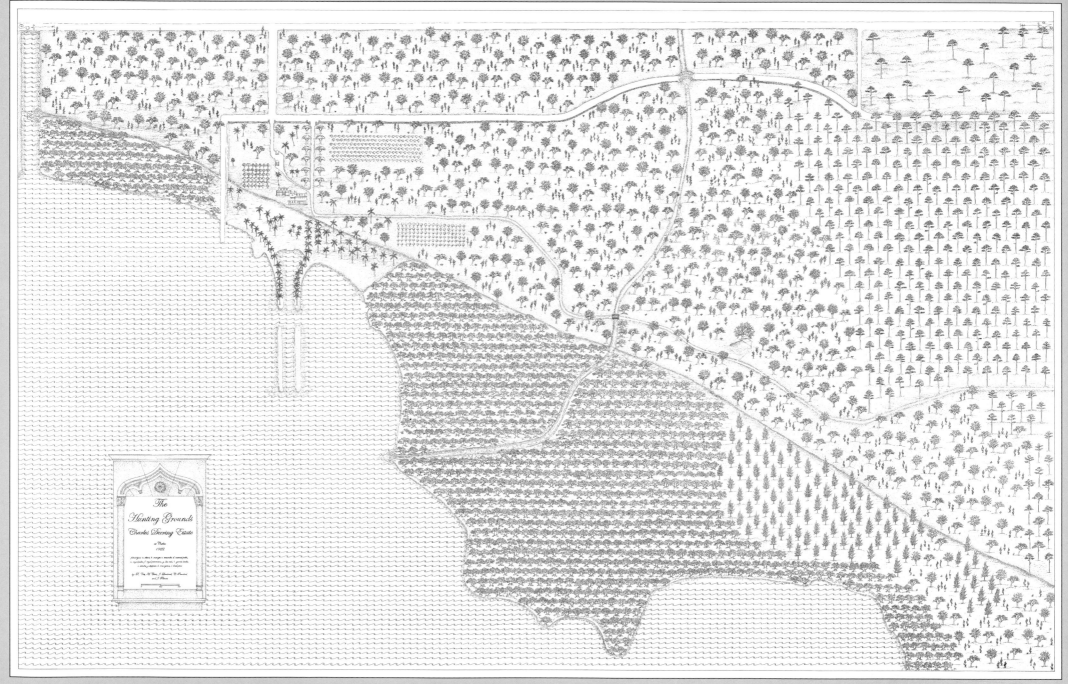

The
Hunting Grounds
Charles Deering Estate
at Cutler
1913

DRAWING BY: R. CEO, ADIB CURE, J. LOMBARD, CARIE PENABAD, JORGE PLANAS
36" X 55", HORIZONTAL FORMAT, INK ON MYLAR, 2001

Charles Deering began assembling the first acreage of his Cutler Estate in 1913. Within two years he had renovated the former Richmond Inn into a family residence and within another seven years built the stone building that would become the main house. During this time he concluded his planting experiments on his first Miami property, Buena Vista, also situated on Biscayne Bay, nearly thirty miles north.[1]

Pavilion photographed by John Kunkel Small, c. 1916.
Historical Museum of Southern Florida.

Charles Deering had made twenty-five acres of the Buena Vista property available to the United States Department of Agriculture for use as a "plant introduction station," and the remaining almost 200 acres supported his own experiments in ornamental plants and crops. As he gradually moved to Cutler full time, his interest in exotic plant materials refocused on the preservation of the native hammock and pinelands. By 1925, after advising David Fairchild, who, with Edward Simmonds, directed the plant introduction station there, the Buena Vista property was sold.[2] In what the *New York Times* called the largest single real estate transaction in the south, the 212 acres brought "a price estimated at $6,080,000."[3] The USDA station moved to Chapman Field and the Deering collection moved to Cutler. According to correspondence between Deering and John Kunkel Small, the noted botanist and curator of the New York Botanical Garden, they had a one-year period after the sale in which to move his most valued plant materials to the Cutler plantation.[4] As the area around Buena Vista had become increasingly urban with the development of Florida East Coast Rail properties, Deering recognized that the Cutler property offered him an opportunity to double his land holdings to support his interest in plant collection and, at the same time, preserve a

View from stone house.
Photograph by D. Hector.

significant natural landscape that was rapidly disappearing from Florida.

Charles Deering's commitment to saving native hammock and pinelands did not end his interest in plant introduction and he developed portions of the Cutler acreage as farmland. To the south he rescued hammock and pineland from a developer's scheme that had platted the area as twenty-four blocks of a subdivision.[5] Charles Torrey Simpson, a noted conchologist and naturalist who retired to Florida and spent the next thirty years describing the plants and animals of southern Florida also wrote *Ornamental Gardening in Florida*, published in 1916. He dedicated this book "To Mr. Charles Deering who, instead of destroying the hammock, is creating it."[6]

It is in the native landscape that the link between Cutler and Vizcaya is evident, as both estates use the hammock and pineland as part of the garden. Although Cutler does not have extensive formal gardens, the bridges, pavilions, and courts provide an opportunity for more detailed design. Photographs of Cutler's landscape during the 1920s made by John Kunkel Small, who collaborated closely with Deering in its shaping, show a grand lawn, encircled by royal palms which frame an opening to a channel leading out to open water. Deering and Small wrote to one another almost daily regarding Small's plant explorations and related planting issues at Cutler. The many photographs Small made of Buena Vista and Cutler record his expansive knowledge of plant life and his interest in the finest scale details.[7]

View from stone house, 1919.
Photograph by John Kunkel Small. Florida State Archives.

As important as John Kunkel Small's role was in the creation of the landscape at Cutler, there is no evidence that he had the strategic thinking that its designer must have commanded. His correspondence with Charles Deering and others involved in the work documents that he made many crucial decisions about what was planted and how it was cultivated. Small's tangential relationship to design is evident in an undated memo headed "Planting at Cutler, Note number 100," that he wrote to J. N. Morrison, the property manager. Small directed Morrison's work in great detail:

> *to get the trails in the old hammock in good condition: I. Clear the paths of snags, projecting roots and loose stones. Cut off all dead or living branches that obstruct the trail or that project enough to strike one in walking. . . eliminate all dead shrubbery and herbs, and remove all such materials to some spot in the hammock out of view and let it decay. Remove dead palmetto leaves. If any rocks have been chipped off and show white instead of the weathered gray, give them a dab of gray paint. In short, clean up the trails, both the ground and the immediate vegetation so that there will be nothing to offend the eye or interfere with walking.*[8]

The design strategies that combine a great open lawn with a long view out over the water would not seem to come from Small. It is possible that the architect Phineas Paist was involved in the shaping of the green and court. When hired in 1922, Paist began the design of the stone building adjacent to the wood frame structure of the former Richmond

Richmond cottage and stone house.
Photograph by D. Hector.

Inn. Paist would later become a primary architect in Coral Gables. An article in *The Herald* of August seventeenth, 1924, "Frank Button, the landscape architect of Coral Gables," lists Button's previous work on "the Charles Deering Estate at Buena Vista and his home at Cutler." No direct evidence clarifying Button's role has emerged.

In July of 1922 Paist mentioned that Deering would discover "from the second story porch of the new house, quite a good vista of the north shore line with a little trimming of the trees immediately in front of the house." In spite of the minor trimming needed to afford the view, Paist noted that "Morrison tells me you want to preserve all of these at present, so this can await your coming."[9] Paist is referring to a secondary view to the north, not the main view to the east, and since Paist's own, later work in Coral Gables relies on Button's larger landscape strategies, it is possible that the framing of the great water view across the lawn may have involved Button.

Where Paist clearly excelled was in the interweaving of local phenomena and historic traditions. The western entrance to the stone house employs the structure of a traditional column order and yet looks to the immediate interests of Deering for the detail. Carved in

"If you are fortunate enough to obtain a piece of virgin hammock, let it alone for a time; study it carefully and learn its beauties, learn to love and fully appreciate it..."
– Simpson

native limestone, are some of the exotic and native creatures that Deering had collected at Buena Vista. A monkey and a pelican adorn the column capitals of the entrance, and an array of actual shells is pressed into the concrete of a vaulted loggia off the library. Just as the shells may represent the study of Deering's friend, Charles Torrey Simpson, the larger concept of the Cutler garden appears to follow the precepts of Simpson's gardening treatise,

Ornamental Gardening in Florida. With few architectural elements and reliance on landscape for effect, the Cutler estate is living evidence of Simpson's advice:

> *If you are fortunate enough to obtain a piece of virgin hammock, let it alone for a time; study it carefully and learn its beauties, learn to love and fully appreciate it and when you are fully acquainted with its weird attractions a path or paths may be carefully cut through it to whatever is of most interest, always leading these trails along the lines of least resistance.*[10]

Simpson suggests that carrying a walk deep into a hammock where one cannot see out "will make the hammock appear much larger than it really is." Here he is following in a secure lineage of garden designers who have used composition and geometry to expand the illusion of space. Simpson also recognizes the time-honored value of contrast when he recommends, adjacent to the dense growth of a hammock, "an open space left in front of the house for a lawn or grass plot." He advises keeping roads and paths away from the center of the lawn, "in fact let it be an uninterrupted sheet of grass if

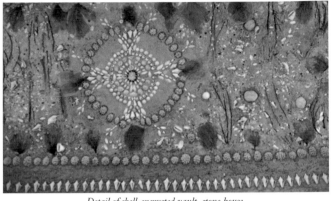
Detail of shell-encrusted vault, stone house.
Photograph by D. Hector.

possible." While Simpson acknowledges the use of a central open space, he is not advocating a formal composition. His ideas are based on the practical understanding of a plant enthusiast for whom the garden is a collection of beloved friends who would not appreciate being cast too rigidly in set roles.

Simpson wrote of his own garden that "the hammock is, by far, the most attractive part." He characterized the hammock as a jungle, the "thing that visitors ask over and rave over." When he was "lonely and depressed" he wandered there "to be alone with nature . . . to let myself become a part and parcel of it all. I feel that the dear trees are my friends and comforters; . . . I always come back to the world and its duties strengthened and refreshed."[11]

"New bridge on west side of Charles Deering's reservation," 1918.
Photograph by John Kunkel Small. Florida State Archives.

Deering's Cutler estate retains the magic of Simpson's hammock. The garden begins in front of the house with the lawn that gives the broad view to the sea, then quickly engages hammock and pineland. Rustic bridges and pathways encourage the visitor to discover plant life in a setting of naturalized forest. The events of the garden are discovered within this wood, and the garden itself gives the impression of having been discovered rather than created.

In 1929, Small published *From Eden to Sahara: Florida's Tragedy.* Before his death two years earlier, Charles Deering had offered to contribute to its publication.[12] For most of its 114 pages, Small documents the geologic conditions and characteristic vegetation of the peninsula. Counterpointing passages that elaborate upon Florida's natural beauty are those that describe the inestimable losses that had occurred during the short intervals between Small's visits.

He reports "wholesale devastation of the plant covering, through carelessness, thoughtlessness, and vandalism."[13] Small decries "the destruction of aboriginal village sites, kitchen-middens, burial mounds, and ceremonial structures." The process of eradication, he says, is "progressing without any attempt at a scientific study and interpretation, not to mention preservation." He finds this destruction astonishing. Florida is one vast "natural history museum" for him, "a unique El Dorado" where the "floristics of temperate, subtropic, and tropic regions not only meet, but mingle; where the animals of temperate regions associate with those of the tropics." He pleads for its preservation "not only for its beauty, but also for its educational value . . . within easy reach of the majority of the population of the United States."[14]

The early depredation of Florida's landscape that Small, Simpson, and Deering deplored and resisted, continued at an increasingly accelerated pace.

Entry, stone house.
Photograph by D. Hector.

Entrance gate at Deering Estate.
Photograph by D. Hector.

Currently, the estates of the Deerings are surrounded by development. Charles Deering's preservation of Cutler's open land has proved to be an immeasurable gift to the future. Since the devastation of Hurricane Andrew in 1992, Miami-Dade County has restored the property and opened the estate to a broad audience. Since then, participation in the life of the Cutler property has both enhanced appreciation for the native landscape and expanded public understanding of the importance of conservation. In this way the county's stewardship has fostered the earliest goals of Deering and his colleagues at the Cutler Estate.

–JL

Notes:

1. Janet Snyder Matthews, *Historical Documentation: The Charles Deering Estate at Cutler*, May 1992, 63.

2. Matthews, 1992, 91; Bertram Zuckerman, *The Kampong: The Fairchild's Tropical Paradise* (National Tropical Botanical Garden and Fairchild Tropical Garden, 1993), 47.

3. "Charles Deering Dies in Florida," *New York Times*, Monday February 7, 1927, 19.

4. Charles Deering to John Kunkel Small, May 31, 1925, Florida State Archive, in Janet Snyder Matthews, *Historical Documentation: The Charles Deering Estate at Cutler*, May 1992, 138.

5. Matthews, 1992, 85.

6. Charles Torrey Simpson, *Ornamental Gardening in Florida* (Little River, Florida, 1916).

7. J.K. Small Collection, Florida Department of State, Division of Library and Information Services, Bureau of Archives and Records Management, online at: http://www.dos.state.fl.us/fpc

8. J. K. Small to J. N. Morrison, Folder 5, Historical Museum of Southern Florida.

9. Paist to Deering, July 10, 1922, Box 4, Charles Deering Photo prints, Historical Museum of Southern Florida.

10. Simpson, 1916, 4.

11. Simpson, 1916, 83.

12. Matthews, 1992, 141.

13. John Kunkel Small, *From Eden to Sahara: Florida's Tragedy* (Lancaster, PA: The Science Press Printing Company, 1929), preface.

14. Small, 1929, 114.

DRAWING BY: F. BURRALL HOFFMAN, JR. OFFICE, VIZCAYA COLLECTION
24" x 36" HORIZONTAL FORMAT, MYLAR REPRODUCTION OF ORIGINAL INK ON LINEN, C.1914

C arved from a dense hammock edged by mangrove and thick with bobcats, land crabs, herons, alligators and swarms of mosquitoes, the Villa Vizcaya proposed an architecture and a landscape that celebrated local materials and still made room for the artifacts and conveniences of civilization. James Deering began the project in 1912, commenced construction in 1914, and opened the house to a close circle of family and friends in late December of 1916. The following year the house and its gardens were featured in an extensive article in *The Architectural Review*, and by 1923 the gardens were complete.

Deering began with 130 acres of mangrove, black marsh, and hammock in northern Coconut Grove and eventually acquired 180 acres.[1] The Villa hosted its own farm, railroad stop, and enough property and staff for both necessities and pleasure. The pleasure grounds not only included the ten acres of gardens closest to the house that are open to the public today, but also an additional seventeen acres of gardens with points of interest scattered throughout the

Postcard showing parterre view looking south, c.1920s.
Florida State Archives.

mangrove and hammock. A series of winding canals and lagoons extended the garden into the wilderness.

Kathryn Harwood sorted through archival materials to reconcile the many conflicting stories that attributed the design of Vizcaya to various figures. She has established the contributions of the three principals who were involved in its creation. Paul Chalfin, Deering's closest advisor, has often been solely credited for the work, but Harwood believes his role was rather that of a director of the works who actively engaged in crucial selections and decisions while he coordinated the work of an architect and a garden designer.[2] Both the decorator Elsie de Wolfe and Isabella Stewart Gardner, the collector whose Boston home is now a museum, recommended Chalfin to Deering. Chalfin, a Harvard graduate and recipient of the *Prix de Rome*, was an accomplished painter and a former curator of the Boston Museum of Fine Arts.[3]

In his role as Deering's artistic advisor, Chalfin was involved in the earliest planning for Vizcaya. He arranged to buy the property from Mary Brickell and acted as Deering's advocate in every regard. Chalfin traveled across Europe with Deering to study precedents and to acquire the

Northern pergola.
Photograph by J. Lombard.

furnishings for Vizcaya.[4] And it was Chalfin who recommended the architect, F. Burrall Hoffman, to Deering. Hoffman had studied at Harvard College and *L'Ecole des Beaux-Arts*. Chalfin had invited Hoffman to lecture in a series arranged at Elsie de Wolfe's request for the Colony Club in New York when Hoffman was working on the Harriman residence there for the firm of Carrère and Hastings.[5] By 1910, Hoffman had founded his own firm with Harry Christian Ingalls, and in 1912, Chalfin asked him to begin work on Vizcaya.[6]

Chalfin also hired Diego Suarez to design the gardens. Suarez had studied engineering in Bogotá until his father's death and then returned with his mother to her native Italy and studied architecture. Suarez originally met Chalfin and Deering at *La Pietra,* the villa and garden of Suarez' friend and mentor, Arthur Acton. In an interview dated 1953, Suarez declared that Acton "should be known to future generations as mainly responsible, together with the great French landscape architect, Achille Duchêne,

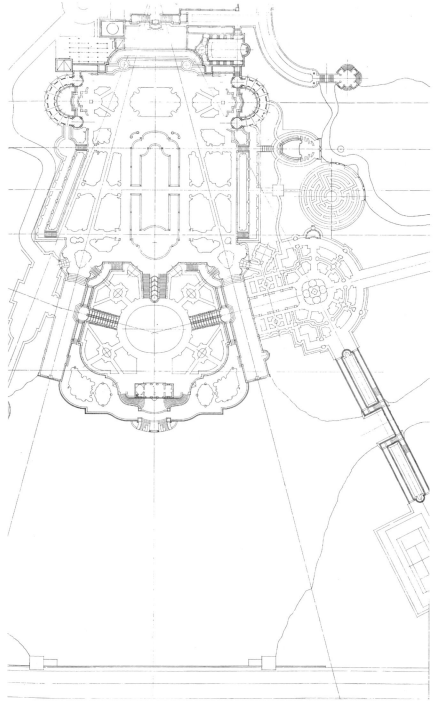

for the revival of the great art of classical design." At Acton's request, Suarez "spent several days showing Mr. Deering and Mr. Chalfin" the gardens of Florence. Then in 1914, Suarez "accidentally met" Chalfin in New York. Shortly thereafter, Suarez began work on the gardens of Vizcaya. Suarez cited the Villa Lante as his original source of inspiration, but told his interviewer that the brilliance of the southern sun provoked new considerations so that he drew upon the "Corsini Villa near Rome," the "grass avenues . . . of Villa Gamberaia in Florence," and numerous Italian gardens for other elements.[7]

Like Villa Lante's original surrounding wood, the tropical hammock, a cool, fragrant network of thin, vertical trunks and delicately scaled foliage, surrounds Vizcaya. Small spots of intense light dapple the ground plane and introduce the Florida sun, opening to an elliptical carriage court that is linked to Vizcaya's entry court with a series of stepped terraces with symmetrical water cascades. The second elliptical forecourt is grander, but still barely permits a single view of the villa facade. The surrounding hammock encloses this court also and its theatrical unveiling is a prelude to the court at the center of the villa as well as to the gardens and bayfront. In 1917, William Patterson, writing in *Town & Country* appreciated the drama:

Progress along the allée, with its low voiced waterways hidden under the Ilex trees is full of the pleasantest surprises. And the climax of the unexpected is in the house itself, which has been carefully screened by the planting and which is finally reached through the iron grilles and open arcades of the first loggia.[8]

That first loggia surrounds one of Vizcaya's most interesting spaces, the central courtyard of the house, originally open to the sky as well as to the eastern loggia that overlooks the bay. It was a lush interior garden where, as Patterson described it,

sounds are heard, remote and nearby, of dropping water, of falling water, of brokenly rushing water in fountains; and glimpses of a gallery beneath broad overhanging roofs give a hint of the importance of the courtyard in plan.[9]

Within the central court, the vista to the bay is finally revealed. The present-day visitor can only imagine the sounds and sensations Patterson

Gazebo view across parterre.
Photograph by J. Lombard.

View of barge, c. 1920s.
Florida State Archive.

described so vividly because the courtyard is now completely enclosed and covered with a glass roof. Through the early 1980s, it was possible to experience the full sensation of the central court and until then, as Patterson had observed in 1917:

the most auspicious hour for a descent into the court is in late afternoon, when a fast deepening yellow light falls on the myriad colors of the old tiled roof and heavy storm clouds may contribute a dramatic background for a tower flushed with sun or between the dimmed colonnades of the gallery the lights from silvered brackets glimmer in the dusk.[10]

On the bay side, a terrace opens as a stage set before the stone barge and together they complete the composition which extends the entry axis out to Biscayne Bay. The barge originally supported a lattice teahouse and garden which gave the barge height and with the

pavilion at the end of the southern arm of the terrace, formed a viewing frame for the central axis that extends to the horizon. Suarez called the barge "the proudest architectural creation of my life," writing that it was "inspired by the famous barge at the Villa Borromeo at Isola Bella on Lago Maggiore in Northern Italy . . . The model was submitted to the distinguished sculptor Sterling Calder for his creation of sculpture to decorate the barge."[11] Period photographs show that the barge was, as Suarez conceived it, an island garden.

Although the barge of today lacks its original vertical dimension, it still is an important foreground to the bay. As an element whose detail gives majesty to an expanse, the barge is part of a long-standing garden tradition. In seventeenth century France, Jacques Boyceau used a similar positioning of elements in order to ". . . allow the spectator measurability both of the whole and its parts."[12]

On the north side of the villa, a rusticated garden with a pergola introduces a small wood.

Postcard postmarked June 22, 1925
Florida State Archive.

Patterson's description of its original form included, ". . . on the north a long turf walk bordered by trees, ambles past ancient statues to the winding of an underwood promenade."[13] A grotto-like pool faces the terrace that borders the pergola garden. Vizcaya's northern wood was relatively untouched, introducing winding paths and canals that traveled "under rustic bridges and past little waterfalls."[14] At the distant reaches, Chalfin planned a village for the staff as

Eastern edge of parterre.
Photograph by J. Lombard.

well as a farm with numerous service buildings detailed as dependencies of an Italian villa.[15]

On the south side of the villa, two raised terraces mark the east and west boundaries of the formal gardens. These gardens are composed of a series of parterres that extend to the southern limit of the formal gardens and finally meet a lake above which the casino is situated. In the *Architectural Review* article on the gardens, Paul Chalfin (or perhaps Diego Suarez who later said that he wrote the article in Chalfin's stead) described the effort "to adapt spaces in the thick forest lying

North face of casino.
Photograph by R. Ceo.

The high mound at the south end of the parterres is formed by "heroic figures," who "guard access to deep grottoes on either side of the cascade, and these shadowed openings are reflected directly upon the water at the extreme end of the great pool."[17] Returning to the main axis that leads out from the center of the southern facade of the house, are "the waters of a great pool ornamented with pyramids and stone vases surround an island lawn, connected by two bridges with the adjacent gardens; further, a Roman cascade, flanked by steps, ascends to the higher end of the terrace."[18] Suarez said that he "made the working drawings for the elaborate boxwood parterres in the main garden, inspired principally by the gardens of the palace of Caserta near Naples."[19] Eventually, the boxwood was replaced by a native jasmine, which provided similar structure and the requisite hardiness.

Diego Suarez described his first encounter with the site when he realized that his use of the

near the house on three sides to form the outer limits of the gardens." The terraces, lateral to the parterres between the house and the high mound towards the lake, stand out against the existing trees.[16]

traditional method of terracing down from the villa to a distant view was entirely wrong. On this tropical site, the visitor looking south was blinded, as the brilliant tropical sun was reflected off the surface of the lake and back to the viewer. Since the entire formal garden would be painful to behold in the dazzling light, Suarez knew that redesign was essential. Years later Suarez explained that:

My new conception consisted principally in the idea of going down from the house terrace to the garden level, and of going up again to a higher level; and in the building of a high mound, crowned by a curtain of high trees between the gardens and the lake . . . However, there remained a very serious problem in connection with my new design and the creation of the mound, viz; the fact that the mound with its high curtain of trees, prevented the sight of the lake from the house.[20]

The challenge of introducing the distant lake to the formal parterres while screening the accompanying, amplified sunlight led Suarez to what he believed was his

most original idea in relation to the Vizcaya gardens; the planning of the gardens and mound in a roughly speaking V shape, flanking the mound by two grass avenues inspired by the Villa Gamberaia in Florence, with a balustrade and a statue in the middle

at the end of each vista, so that one could have a glimpse of the lake from the house.[21]

Atop the mound, Suarez placed the casino, composed of two "small cabinets, decorated in taste of the eighteenth century," offering a "refuge from the tropical day."[22] This little building resembles the Farnese casino at Caprarola in its tripartite organization of two rooms flanking a central, open pavilion, and in its position at the head of the water stair.

East facade viewed from the bay with teahouse on barge, c. 1920s.
Photograph by W.A. Fishbaugh. Florida State Archive.

The northern face of the casino looks back at the villa across an elliptical lawn and permits baroque vistas of the garden rooms along the eastern edge of the parterres. The southern face meets a cascading stair that leads to a lower lawn

View across parterre from casino.
Photograph by J. Lombard.

bordered by the lake. Originally, the lower lawn also led southeast to a bridge lined with palms, that in turn framed a vista into the wood, where a network of small canals and waterways surrounded several islands. The islands housed the recreational pieces of the garden, including tennis courts and a boathouse, as well as ornamental pieces, including the Casbah, an Arabian nights inspired pavilion and fish garden.

Central courtyard, 1980.
Photograph by J. Lombard.

Renaissance gardens often evoked the Golden Age of classical mythology. The sixteenth century Villa D'Este in Tivoli, Italy, for example, recalls episodes from the life of Hercules, a series of heroic events grown from an oral tradition to an epic tale well known to the garden's visitors.[23] Vizcaya calls to mind a golden memory of Europe, a specific and personal journey into the interests of James Deering. Instead of enacting a unified program of classical allusion, Vizcaya tells the story of its tropical situation. Deering, Chalfin, Hoffman, and Suarez employed sophisticated and learned design strategies to create the extraordinary estate of Vizcaya. They evoked precedents distant in time and space even while they refined the garden's focus on the immediate Florida landscape and its unique and threatened beauties. The resulting landscape of Vizcaya achieved a remarkable integration of profound ideas that span time and place with materials and details that dramatize its tropical site.

–JL

Notes:

1. James T. Maher, *The Twilight of Splendor* (Boston and Toronto: Little, Brown and Company, 1975), 164.

2. Kathryn Chapman Harwood, *The Lives of Vizcaya* (Miami: Banyan Press 1985), 10.

3. Maher, 172.

4. Harwood, 8-10.

5. Maher, 174.

6. Maher 172-80.

7. Diego Suarez, Untitled recollection on the design of the gardens, 1953, Vizcaya Archive 2.

8. William Patterson, "A Florida Echo of the Glory of Old Venice," *Town & Country* (July 20, 1917), 24.

9. Patterson, 24.

10. Patterson, 30.

11. Suarez, 1953, 7.

12. Franklin Hamilton Hazlehurst, *Jacques Boyceau and the French Formal Garden* (Athens: Univ. of Georgia Press, 1966), 88.

13. Patterson, 24.

14. Patterson, 28.

15. "Vizcaya," *Harper's Bazaar* (July 1917): 41.

16. "Vizcaya, the Villa and Grounds," *The Architectural Review* 5, no. 7 (July 1917): 121-140.

17. *Architectural Review*, 1917, 123.

18. *Architectural Review*, 1917, 123.

19. Suarez, 1953, 8.

20. Suarez, 1953, 8.

21. Suarez, 1953, 8.

22. *Architectural Review*, 1917, 123.

23. David Coffin, *The Villa in the Life of Renaissance Rome*, (Princeton: Princeton University Press [1979] 1988), 329.

Henry Ford Winter Residence
2350 McGregor Boulevard, Fort Myers, FL 33901
— 1915 —

DRAWING BY: VALERY AUGUSTIN, JOSE BOFILL
20" X 42", VERTICAL FORMAT, INK ON MYLAR, 1995

He [John Burroughs] criticized industrial progress, and he declared that the automobile was going to kill the appreciation of nature. I fundamentally disagreed with him. I thought that his emotions had taken him on the wrong tack and so I sent him an automobile with the request that he try it out and discover for himself whether it would not help him to know nature better. That automobile – and it took him some time to learn how to manage it himself – completely changed his point of view.[1]

– Henry Ford writing about the naturalist John Burroughs.

It seems only fitting that the man who revolutionized the production of automobiles so that nearly everybody could own one, should have chosen in 1916 to make an automobile entrance the principal one to his winter residence in Fort Myers. His doing so marked a significant departure from the standard practice of approaching houses from the Caloosahatchee River, a pattern that had prevailed in the town since its early years. This shift in site orientation away from the water, a shift generated by the building of trains and the use of the automobile, was of course to have a profound effect on Florida's gardens of every description. It dictated that such houses as Ford's have two fronts and that their grounds must also present two faces to the world. Ford's house marks the beginning of a new preference for the development of architecture and gardens that turn their principal elevations to the street instead of the water.

Ford first came to Florida at the invitation of Thomas Edison, who asked him to tour the Everglades and cypress forests in the southern part of the state. Their companion on the trip was the naturalist John Burroughs whose newfound enthusiasm for tropical flora and fauna proved infectious. The trip apparently sold Ford on the idea that he needed a residence in Florida. In December 1916, Ford purchased for $20,000 dollars a plot of three and a half acres beside the home of his former employer and friend Thomas Edison. The two men had made many cross-country trips together, and in California they had traveled by automobile caravan from Riverside to San Diego. Living side by side could recapture something of those good times.

Palm allée.
Photograph by R. Ceo.

Although Ford soon made improvements to the house, built in 1911 by Robert W. Smith, a New York financier, it had been well outfitted before he arrived. Within its two-story wood frame there were fourteen rooms and a large detached garage. The house sat within a grove of grapefruit, orange, and mango trees and on its water side there were stands of bamboo and coconut palms, no doubt the product of Edison's cultivation next-door.

Smith's house was well suited to the Ford's needs, with an open living room for Henry and Clara's passion for square dancing and a second floor porch off the master bedroom that afforded good views of the palm allée, and the

Caloosahatchee beyond. Strong twin dormers that punctuate both sides of the gable roof assist

Postcard, Rocco Ceo Collection.

in framing formal axes from the house to the water and from the house to the road. The house sits on this axis in a rather simple straight-forward way, so that approaches from the water and from the street appear similar.

However, the site had four entrances. By foot one can take an axial path from MacGregor Boulevard (then called Riverside Drive) to the front door, or choose another footpath from the Edison House that entered through a gate in the fence under a big Moreton Bay Fig. This tree (now gone) straddled the lot line between Ford's and Edison's houses and, with its buttressing roots, joined the two sites. By automobile one can wind through the grove to the garage. From a boat, visitors disembarked at a long dock from the Caloosahatchee River and proceeded to a

bamboo landing that marks the entrance to an allée of royal palms axially aligned with the back porch. The house in the grove reflects Ford's understanding of the world. His house was a place of action, and of work as well as pleasure. In his 1922 autobiography, Ford shares his pragmatic view of nature: "The foundations of society are the men and means to *grow* things, to *make* things, and to *carry* things. As long as agriculture, manufacture, and transportation survive, the world can survive any economic or social change." [2]

The Ford landscape has a Cartesian order to its plantings and choice of species. Ford believed in simplicity. He believed that the land should be serviceable and functional. The absence of decorative plantings and the accessibility of the landscape were consistent with Ford's understanding that reconciled his admiration of Burrough's ideas with the use of the automobile. Nature was to be accessible; it was now possible to see more. And this idea might have appealed to Burroughs, especially in his later years when he probably appreciated being able to ride into an often-dense landscape.

Both the reorientation of Ford's house and John Burrough's having "completely changed his point of view" about the relationship between nature and the automobile were prophetic of just how radically and fundamentally Ford's product would re-orient perception of Florida's landscape. Even though he recognized something of the automobile's destructive potential, Burroughs, one of the greatest naturalists of his day, apparently came to value the automobile for its ability to transport him into the heart of nature.

Mysore fig tree (Ficus mysorensis).
Photograph by R. Ceo.

Citrus grove.
Photograph by R. Ceo.

But the automobile wrought even more radical changes that have altered our very consciousness of the Florida landscape. The new orientation to the street instead of the water marks a new visual understanding of Florida, one in which the dominance of the view of land seen from

Postcard, Rocco Ceo Collection.

water as object or shoreline is gone forever. Embedded into a landscape now opened for trains and automobiles, settlers in Florida would expand the clearings to accomodate a new vision, in which human dominance over the land would become the most conspicuous feature.

–RJC

Notes:

1. Henry Ford, *My Life and Work* (Garden City, New York, 1922), 237.

2. Ford, 1922, 7.

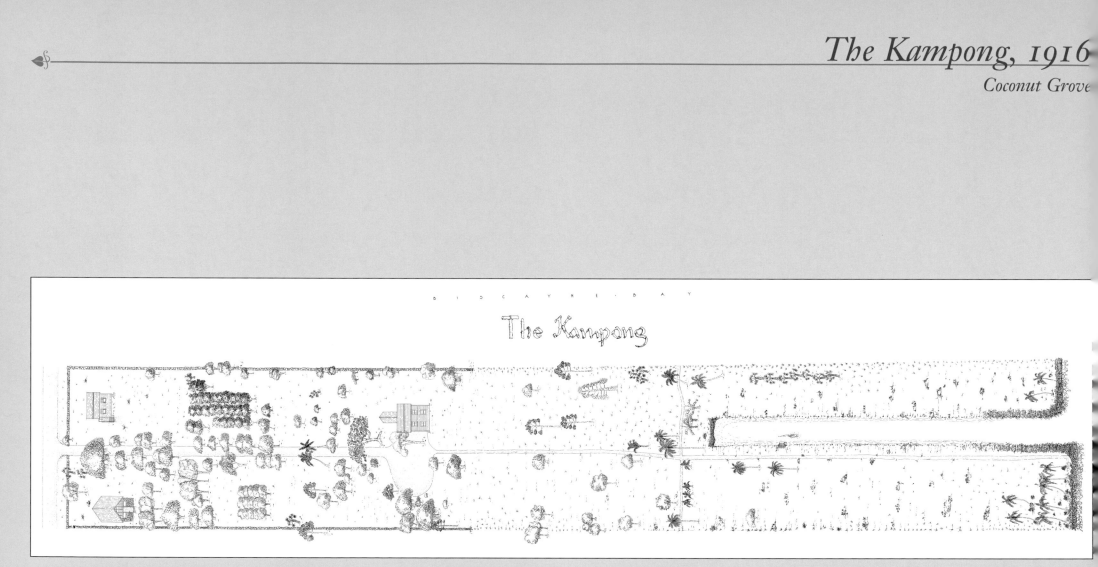

BISCAYNE BAY

The Kampong

DRAWING BY: ALISA BLOCK, BEATRIZ HERNANDEZ
22½" X 73¾", VERTICAL FORMAT, INK ON MYLAR, 1992

Detail of drawing.

O n February 16, 1916, David and Marian Fairchild decided to buy one of the few properties available on the Atlantic coastal ridge overlooking Biscayne Bay. David Fairchild was the famed plant explorer who had helped initiate the United States Department of Agriculture's first Office of Foreign Seed and Plant Introduction in Washington, D.C. in 1893. Fairchild held a leadership position there from 1906 until his retirement in 1928 during which time his expeditions were responsible for the introduction of "approximately 75,000 selected varieties and species of useful plants into the United States," including "such widely grown crops as Duram wheat, Japanese rice, date Palms, Sudan grass, Chinese soy beans, Siberian and Peruvian alfalfa, Chinese elms, velvet beans, persimmons, pistachios, Central American avocados and a host of other important crop plants."[1]

Marian Fairchild was the daughter of Alexander Graham Bell, best known for his invention of the telephone, and Mary Hubbard, daughter of telephone investor Gardiner Greene Hubbard, founding member and first president of the National Geographic Society. Marian Fairchild had studied sculpture with Gutzon Borglum, now recognized for his work at Mount Rushmore, and through her studies became friends with Clarence Dean, the architect who later would design The Kampong as well as the Fairchild's summer house in Nova Scotia.[2]

Although Fairchild may have sought a place of his own in Florida where he could work with the plants that absorbed his interest, he described the decision to buy the Nugent property on Biscayne Bay as a "hurricane move on Marian's part."[3] Ten days after seeing the property and receiving the approval and funding from Marian

Channel from Biscayne Bay.
Photograph by R. Ceo.

Fairchild's mother, Mrs. Bell, David Fairchild revisited the property, deliberately alone in order to preserve memories that he "believed would be sacred for the rest of my days."

"All up the gentle slope to the doorstep of the house the ground was covered with a collection of those charming wild-flowers…"

– David Fairchild

He "walked down the narrow white road under the mangos and strolled about among the grapefruit trees that were loaded with fruits, and looked at the undersides of the leaves of a lot of guava bushes which were covered with white fly."[4]

He bought the property from Mrs. Nugent, although its history was unknown to him on that day. Fairchild later learned that a previous owner, Dr. Galt Simmons, had been a country doctor who ministered to the settlers as well as the natives. She had been "a remarkable woman, a graduate of Bryn Mawr, who with her husband, Captain Simmons, lived here and loved this place."[5] He discovered tamarinds and a Geiger tree, as well as a frame house built of Dade County pine with an oolitic limestone fireplace.[6]

Eventually the wood-frame house would be moved elsewhere on the property to accommodate a larger house, but in his earliest moments at The Kampong, the house and its history appealed to Fairchild. He:

Entrance gate with view of Biscayne Bay.
Photograph by R. Ceo.

sat for a long time that morning gazing out to sea, and at the beach of coral and limestone and the low land back of it which was beginning to be covered with all sorts of wild vegetation. Some small mangrove trees had already established themselves at the entrance to a canal that led from the bay to the group of royal palms, the palms that Mrs. Nugent had planted and had pointed out to us in the distance when we first visited the place . . . All up the gentle slope to the doorstep of the house the ground was covered with a collection of those charming wild-flowers which made the meadow-like front yards of the early settlers here on the bay things of delicate beauty.[7]

Reflecting on the panorama, Fairchild marked the moment, perceiving:

this was a paradise of plants, not one of oriental divans and swimming pools and cushions and dancing girls. It was another kind of paradise, appealing to a different side of our natures, one that had been fed by visits to the museums of art in Europe and by the landscape beauties of the Alps, the coral beaches of the Pacific, the jungled overhead tangles of vegetation of the rivers of Florida, and those incomparable tropical gardens where I had studied, at various places around the world.[8]

The plants, sea, and skyscape formed the significant outer architecture of the property within which the Fairchilds began to rearrange, rebuild, and build freshly a domestic architecture to accommodate the changing needs of their life and work. With the artistic eye of Marian Fairchild, and the guidance and design skills of her friend and architect Clarence Dean, the compound took shape. In 1928 they built the main house that remains on the property, with its distinctive arched gateway that frames the vista to the bay. Fairchild explained that the name of the property evolved as the buildings took shape. "By the time we finished putting up houses and moving shacks about," Fairchild noted, "there were so many buildings on the place that it suggested a little village —a Javanese Kampong, and 'The Kampong' it became."[9]

This architecture, drawn from native materials, remains the backdrop and frame. The actors on the stage of The Kampong are the plants, native and exotic, that served to test Fairchild's theories on how various plants would grow in Florida and what new hybrids might be developed. Fairchild describes many failed experiments, including those with plants that voraciously acquired real estate at the expense of their neighbors. In fact, he explains in the book he devoted to describing The Kampong that "one of the chief objects of this story is to picture this bit of land – two hundred feet wide and eighteen hundred feet long, running from the highway down to the shore – as the scene of a pastoral drama in which the characters change so vastly that any producer would be baffled completely."[10]

Considering the change that occurs as an aspect of time and care, Fairchild recalled that:

Mrs. Charles Torrey Simpson once determined for me all the beautiful, delicate annuals and perennials which flowered among the tufts of wiry native grasses on the rocky slope leading down from our front terrace to the shore. We planned to keep this foreground in its original state, but we had an inadequate idea of the forces against us. Long absences and busy days

Front door.
Photograph by R. Ceo.

Entrance from bay.
Photograph by R. Ceo.

on our part have resulted in the overgrowth of the native flora by all sorts of strangers, some of my own introducing. A spindling little thing not two feet high has grown into a giant Ficus benjamina . . . *A small piece of a bromeliad,* Hohenbergia distans, *given me by Professor Simpson, who was proud to have collected it in western Cuba, has become as large as an eagle's nest in the branches of a live oak where I fastened it years ago; while a tall grass from Madagascar, something like Pampas grass, called "Fantaka"–*Neyraudia arundinacea *– and used by the natives to make hats, has invaded the southern part of the area. But at least it is still untamed.*[11]

His explorations took him across the globe and in particular into "untamed" landscapes. While the Fairchilds had homes in Chevy Chase and Baddeck, Nova Scotia, The Kampong remained the most tangible link between this scientist's professional interests and his domestic life.

In 1963, Catherine (Kay) and Edward Sweeney acquired the property from the Fairchild heirs. Until 1984, Kay Sweeney maintained The Kampong "to promote work in horticulture, to provide a valuable germ plasm resource and to preserve the property for posterity."[12]

Then, in 1984, she gave the property to what is now the National Tropical Botanical Garden, an institution with four gardens and three preserves in Hawaii. The National Tropical Botanical Garden through its work in Hawaii and at The Kampong is dedicated to the conservation of tropical plant diversity, with a focus on rare and endangered species, a goal worthy of David Fairchild's home.

–JL

State champion Royal poinciana tree.
Photograph by R. Ceo.

Notes:

1. Bertram Zuckerman, *The Kampong: The Fairchilds' Tropical Paradise* (Miami: National Tropical Botanical Garden and Fairchild Tropical Garden, 1993), 33.

2. Zuckerman, 1993:40.

3. David Fairchild, *The World Grows Round My Door*, (New York and London: Charles Scribner's Sons, 1947), 26.

4. Fairchild, 1947, 27.

5. Fairchild, 1947, 29.

6. Fairchild, 1947, 30.

7. Fairchild, 1947, 32.

8. Fairchild, 1947, 33.

9. Fairchild, 1947, 39.

10. Fairchild, 1947, 40.

11. Fairchild, 1947, 46-7.

12. Zuckerman, 1993, 142.

Drawing by: Kristine Colunga, Philip Smith, Adam Rydzewski
18" x 69", vertical format, ink on vellum, 1996

El Jardin takes inspiration from Italian villas of the Renaissance with their woods and gardens in which dependent buildings, including gatehouses, lodges and carriage houses were assembled and views to the distant landscape were composed. James Deering recreated all these elements on almost 200 hundred acres at Villa Vizcaya. Just a few miles south, John Bindley, then president of Pittsburgh Steel, built El Jardin in 1918, on a more modest bayfront property of ten acres, but his architect, Richard Kiehnel, was able to achieve many of the grand gestures that were so effective at Vizcaya.

Born and educated in Germany, Kiehnel lived in Chicago, Cleveland and then Pittsburgh where he met Bindley. Kiehnel moved to Florida to design and supervise the construction of El Jardin and later built a productive practice that drew upon a variety of architectural styles.[1] Although El Jardin's courtyard organization recalls Mediterranean examples, the rooms of the villa reflect Kiehnel's broad repertory, which includes references to the nineteenth century English country house. The English model that places gardens close to the formal rooms of a house, with a deer park beyond, served him at El Jardin. Although the wildlife is limited to an occasional fox, the depth of the property, spanning almost sixteen-hundred feet from Biscayne Bay to Coconut Grove's Main Highway, still gives some illusion of a wooded context.

The villa occupies the edge of a limestone promontory nearly a thousand feet from the water. The gardens closest to the house introduce exotic palms to frame views, while the perimeter of the property reverts to the native pineland and hammock. To achieve the refined finishes of the villa, John B. Orr, the contractor who built El Jardin, was able to engage craftsmen who had completed work at Vizcaya.[2]

The architectural firm of Kiehnel and Elliott, in a monograph on its work that was published in

Entry drive.
Carrollton School Collection.

1938, prominently featured El Jardin.[3] The illustrations of that era reveal a landscape still rich in native materials and show the villa surrounded by slash pine (*Pinus elliottii*, the source of the famed "Dade County Pine"), which filters through the rich hammock that then covered much of Coconut Grove. Period photographs also show the vista to the bay from the eastern face of the villa framed by rows of coconut palms and royal palms that mark the boundaries between the formal grounds and the pineland. El Jardin's rusticated gatehouse with its rough-cut oolitic limestone base, picturesque roofline, and thick timbers suggestive of a country lodge, sits at the western edge of the property, along Main Highway. The road at that time ran through what was still pine rocklands and tropical hardwood hammock, so the image of a sylvan outpost was particularly appropriate.

Bayfront facade.
Carrollton School Collection.

Lattice plant house.
Carrollton School Collection.

A lattice plant house, similar to the tea house on the barge at Vizcaya, framed a view across the property, through a small formal garden, to a composition of Italian cypress trees planted in rows that flanked two stone lanterns and an apse-shaped seating area. Just beyond the plant house,

nearer the villa, Kiehnel placed the carriage house, recalling Richard Morris Hunt's siting of Vanderbilt's carriage houses at Biltmore. In both cases the carriage house blocks northern winds and creates a protected green for exotic plants.

The detailing of El Jardin's carriage house is more refined than the ornamental program of its gate house. The carriage house façade, a tripartite composition, accommodates three vehicles below and staff quarters above. The upper corners of the building were framed with open porches, while the upper windows are marked with cast concrete lintels and sills. That the carriage house is less ornate than the villa itself is indicative of both its utilitarian function and its position on the site, acting as a barrier and also a bridge between wood and garden. Although it is placed within the boundaries of the compound reserved for culture and civility, the carriage house has a lesser status than the villa, and that is acknowledged in its detailing.

Kiehnel went directly to the villas along the Brenta for his model for the main house of El Jardin. Those villas typically were organized around an open courtyard from which a view

Central courtyard.
Carrollton School Collection.

of the water was revealed. The courtyard in Florida looked through the living room on the first floor and an open porch on the second floor to an expansive view of Biscayne Bay. Within the court, potted palms and pairs of tree-ferns surrounded a central fountain to establish a lush, tropical center for the house.

Kiehnel referred to well known Renaissance themes in the ornamental motifs. Cavorting dolphins and winged creatures adorn the friezes of El Jardin as they had the Renaissance villas, including the Villa Lante in Bagnaia. The Renaissance ornamentation often referred to a mythological origin that corresponded to the iconography of the garden. In the Villa Lante, the dolphins refer to the flood described in Ovid's *Metamorphoses*.[4] The use of the oak leaf,

Pool with bay vista.
Carrollton School Collection.

Entrance with cast ornamentation.
Carrollton School Collection.

the tree of Zeus, as well as the cornucopias of Zeus, and related mythological creatures connected the Bindley family with an ennobled tradition.

The versatility of the themes so fundamental to western culture permit the current life of the estate as Carrollton School of the Sacred Heart to connect those same ornamental themes to its own iconographical tradition of the Duchesne oaks that memorialize one of the Society of the Sacred Heart's pioneering members.

Each building on the property plays a role in the landscape to support the larger goal of El Jardin,

to adapt historical precedents to local conditions. Together, the buildings and landscape elements create a tropical villa set within a pine rockland. The estate offers tangible evidence of the grand aspirations of Florida's early residents and the designers they engaged, to carry forward a long line of architectural and landscape tradition that finds new expression in the tropical bosque.

–JL

Notes:

1. Beth Dunlop, "Inventing Antiquity: The Art and Craft of Mediterranean Revival Architecture," *Florida Theme Issue: The Journal of the Decorative and Propaganda Arts 1875-1945*, 23 (1998): 198.

2. Ivan Rodriguez and Margot Ammidown, *From Wilderness to Metropolis: The History and Architecture of Dade County, Florida 1825-1940* (Miami: Metropolitan Dade County, 1982), 89-90.

3. *A Monograph of the Florida Work of Kiehnel & Elliott Architects* (Miami, 1938), 2-5.

4. David Coffin, *The Villa in the Life of Renaissance Rome* (Princeton: Princeton University Press [1979] 1988), 358.

Main Highway gate and gatehouse.
Carrollton School Collection.

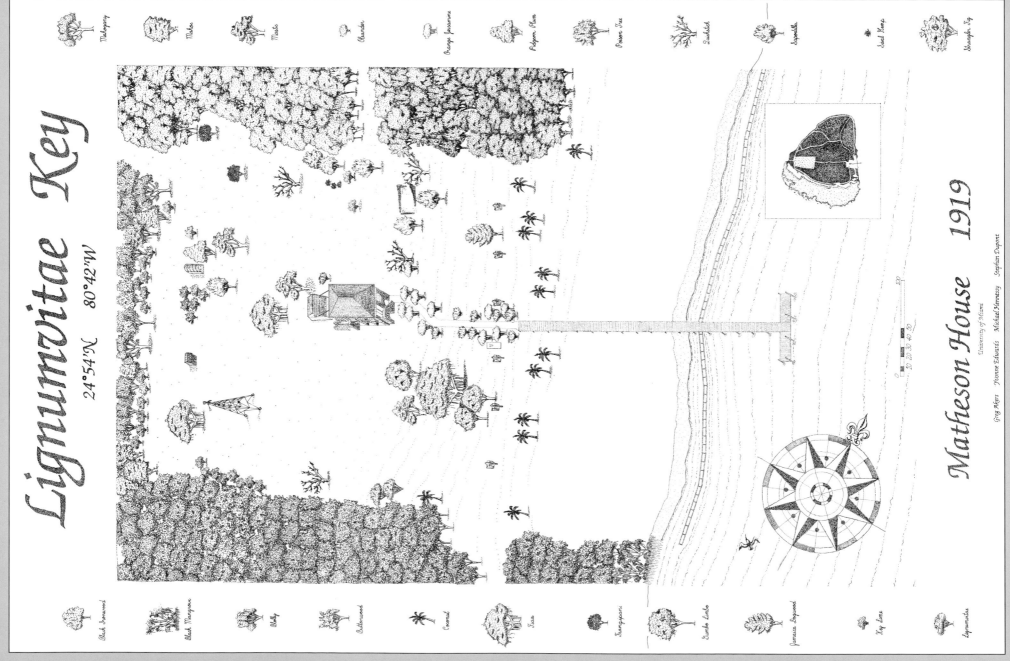

Lignumvitae Key

24°54″N 80°42″W

Matheson House 1919

University of Miami

Greg Akers Yvonne Edwards Michael Hennessy Stephan Dupont

DRAWING BY: GREG AKERS, YVONNE EDWARDS, MICHAEL HENNESSY, STEPHAN DUPONT
24″ x 36″, VERTICAL FORMAT, INK ON MYLAR, 1995

This state park is an entire island that gets its name from its most distinctive feature, the largest stand of lignum vitae trees in North America. Lignum vitae, the common name for the tree, translates to mean "wood of life." Its scientific name is *Guaiacum sanctum*: Guaiac refers to the resinous gum which makes up thirty percent of the tree's weight, while sanctum (Latin for "holy"), alludes to the belief that its wood was used to fashion the Holy Grail. This wood is resinous

Gumbo limbo in hammock.
Photograph by R. Ceo.

and dense, weighing eighty pounds per cubic foot. The density combined with self-lubricating qualities made it ideal for use in the stern tube propeller shaft bearings of World War II Liberty ships. This and many other uses of lignum vitae trees, which were in limited supply, led to their being harvested nearly out of existence. This island is the last place in North America where large specimens still exist in great numbers.

The island that bears the name of these trees rises as high as sixteen feet above sea level within its 345 acres, making it one of the highest points in the Keys, and it also has fresh water wells. These natural features have made Lignumvitae Island a place continually, although minimally, inhabited for centuries. We know that it was once home to Indian populations because of the presence of a burial mound and of seasonal shell refuse deposited as a kitchen midden by Indians who camped there. There is also an impressive, dry-stacked oolitic limestone wall 3000 feet long on the northwest tip of the island. Although the wall is believed to have been built by Caloosa Indians under the direction of Spanish explorers, there is little evidence

Lignum vitae tree along trail.
Photograph by R. Ceo.

to support this claim and its origins remain unexplained.

The range of trees, representing over 140 species, is notable, as are the subtle changes in the types of landscape visible on a path that is only two hundred feet long but drops ten feet in elevation within that short distance. Because of the sharp drop, the walk reveals an unusual variety of native species and plant communities. The island also is home to some of the largest native plants in the country, ones that appear on the National Big Tree Register. They include a mastic tree 102 inches in circumference, a torchwood sixteen inches in circumference, a black mangrove over sixty-four inches in circumference, and a lignum vitae nearly thirty-five inches in circumference.

Aerial view of caretaker house and dock.
Monroe County Library Collection.

Specimens of such trees rarely attain circumferences exceeding ten to fifteen inches, even over many years of growth.[1]

In the early 1800s the island was cultivated by plant explorers and pioneers. Henry Perrine, who brought specimens from Mexico for cultivation and established experimental gardens on nearby Indian Key, was perhaps instrumental in introducing non-native species to Lignumvitae Key as well. His activities were noted in Jefferson B. Browne's book, *Key West: The Old and the New.* Published in 1912, Browne wrote that: "Dr. Perrine brought plants and seeds from Mexico and Central and South America, which he planted on Matecumbe and Lignumvitae Key as nurseries for his mainland colony when the war should end."[2]

Jacob Housman, a wrecker by trade, is also thought to have grown coffee beans there in the mid nineteenth century. This island has had a series of owners. William A. Bethel purchased it in 1881 for $170.32, and in the early 1900s W.J. Matheson owned it for several years.

From Matheson's era, a small caretaker's house, usually characterized as "the coral rock house" survives. It is an excellent example of what it meant to live in the drought- and hurricane-prone keys. Rainwater was collected from the roof of the caretaker's house and was stored in a 12,000 gallon cistern to the rear. Built in a clearing, the main floor is raised ten feet above the ground on a bluff that stands ten feet above sea level on the windward side of the island. This siting assisted in capturing natural breezes to cool the house and protect it from tidal surges and mosquitoes.

Clearing the land around the house was an effective way to facilitate the circulation of air, suppressing collection of mosquitoes. The thick coral rock walls, deep overhangs, hip roof and heavy wood shutters offer protection from the high winds and the driving rains of hurricanes. A Jacobs wind generator provided electrical power, which was stored in glass-celled batteries.

In the late 1930s, the WPA guide to the "Southern-most State" listed the island as a point of interest on a tour, noting that:

On Lignumvitae Key (accessible only by boat), 2 miles west of Upper Matecumbe, are stone fences, wells, pieces of carved wood and wrought iron, the ruins of what is believed by some to have been a Spanish Village. The island is bright with sea lavender (Limonium braseliense), with myriads of rose-colored flowers, and a native leadwort (Plumbago scandens), which sprawls over rocks and shrubs and bears clusters of large pale flowers.[3]

Caretaker house.
Photograph by R. Ceo.

Drawing detail showing house and cistern.

The island is still only accessible by boat, but the trip is well worth it to see the botanical wonders and the evocative remnants of Florida island living a hundred years ago.

–RJC

Notes:

1. Jefferson B. Browne, *Key West: The Old and The New*, Facsimile ed. (1912: Gainesville: University Press of Florida, 1973), 86.

2. Browne, 1973, 86.

3. *Florida: A Guide to the Southernmost State* (New York: Oxford University Press, 1939), 331.

Cistern for rainwater from roof.
Photograph by R. Ceo.

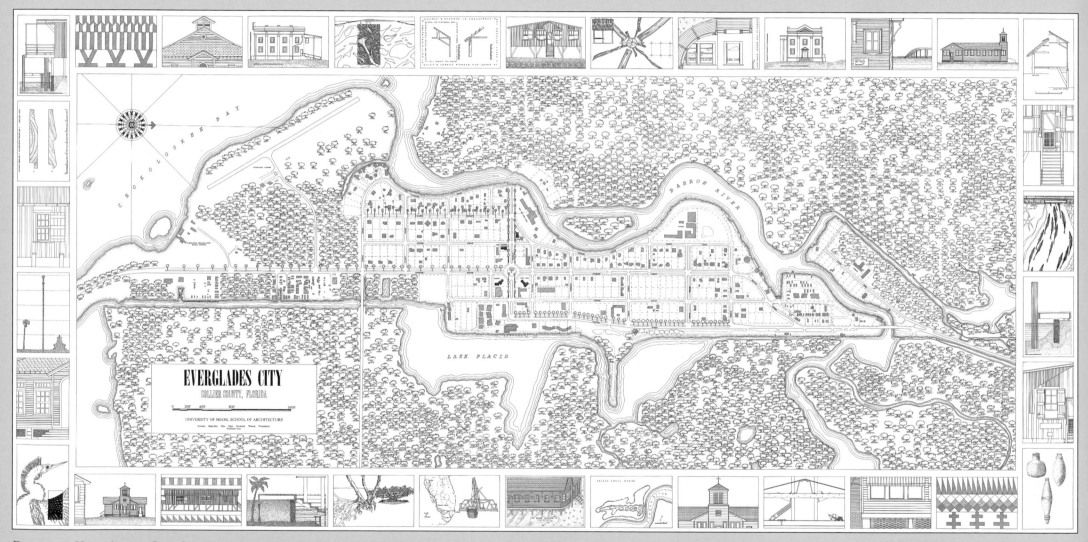

EVERGLADES CITY
COLLIER COUNTY, FLORIDA

0   200'   400'   800'   1600'

UNIVERSITY OF MIAMI SCHOOL OF ARCHITECTURE

Drawing by: Vivian Alvarez, Sonia Baltodano, Yvonne Bianchini, Carlos Chiu, Hao Shan, David Swetland, Frank Wenzel, Gary Wunderlich
36" x 73 1/2", horizontal format, ink on mylar, 1996

Everglades City is a monument to industry and creative advertising. It is a company town sited on fill pumped from the adjacent Barron River by massive dredging undertaken by Barron Collier, a former advertising executive and industrious businessman from Tennessee. He created the town in 1926 as a base camp for the construction of the Tamiami Trail, the road that connected Tampa on the west coast of Florida to Miami on the east.

City Hall.
Photograph by R. Ceo.

If there is such a thing as a landscape made by an act of displacement, it is Everglades City. In building this town that he called simply "Everglade," Collier totally transformed the environment that had been on the site. His act ranks as one of a vandal in the thinking of the present era that has benefited from decades of consciousness-raising about the value of Florida's wetlands. But in Collier's day it was standard operating practice. It perfectly reflected early attitudes toward the Everglades: They were worthless and dangerous swamps, not the "River of Grass" that Marjory Stoneman Douglas taught her readers to appreciate. Collier's contemporaries looked at the Everglades and saw potential agricultural land, or lots ripe for development, if only they could just figure out how to drain it.

Rather than drain, more commonly they dredged. This created better access because it left deep channels for boats while providing land for the construction of roads and home sites. This is how the land for Collier's "Everglade" was created, and its landscape after dredging was one that supported only sparse growth under the baking sun, growth that offered a strong contrast to the thousands of mangrove islands south of the town.

The town's network of streets is based on the original sectional divisions of the site, making

Bank of Everglade with Washingtonia palm.
Photograph by R. Ceo.

the history of the parceling out of land visually present. The roads act like levees and are shot through with culverts that during the rainy season distribute the sixty inches of rain that falls annually. Most buildings sit high on concrete piles or wood piers. The houses, most of which are small, are sheathed in screens to

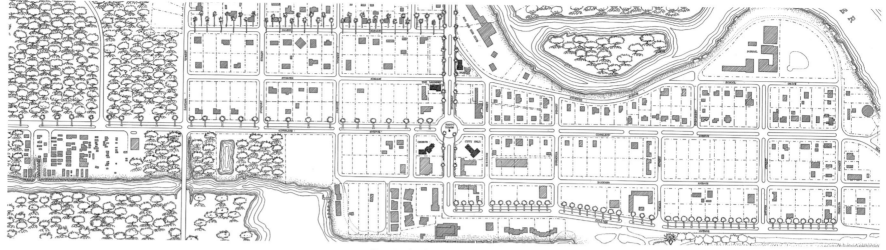

Drawing detail showing center of town.

protect the few who brave the mosquito laden rainy season. Historically, most who settled here came for fish, for sponge, or to participate in all activities associated with the local waters. Residents tended to be close to the water on what is currently the edge of town, but was once the town's main street. The town is therefore built out with the greatest density on the edges, near the water, while the center is relatively vacant except for its public buildings.

The town had a streetcar system even before there was a road into the town. The streetcar was free

Telephone & Radio Tower.
Photograph by R. Ceo.

to all and carried advertisements even though the town was easily walkable and was really not drawing business from anywhere except the residences, which were few in number. The town's most conspicuous feature, a radio tower, conforms to the pattern of striking difference. From Tamiami Trail the presence of Everglades City is first signaled by the appearance of the faint line of a radio tower seen from some distance over an expanse of sawgrass and mangrove. Arriving in the center of town, the tower is geometrically centered in a traffic circle that is bordered by public buildings.

Its prominence as the principal civic monument is indeed appropriate for a town isolated in a landscape as vast as the Everglades. Stretching out from this center in simple regularity, at a lower elevation, are streets lined with very tall *Washingtonia robusta* and sabal palms that create dignified public spaces.

Rod & Gun Club.
Photograph by R. Ceo.

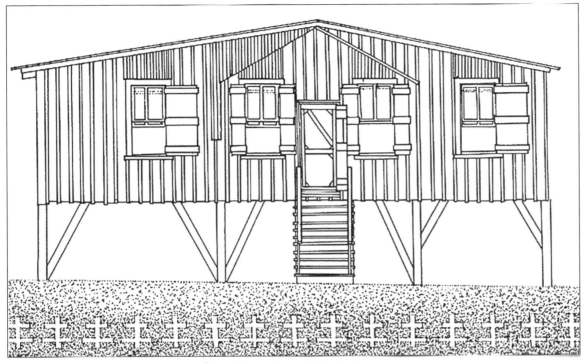

Detail of drawing showing Ted Smallwood's store.

The striking effect of the stark landscape, like the plan of the town, is one of contrast. From the vantage point of the watery landscape of the ten thousand islands to the south of town, an area totally confusing to anyone except those who frequent their tangled irregularities, one can most fully appreciate the Cartesian simplicity and openness of the geometric town plan. This unique townscape is Everglades City, a place of will and fill.

– RJC

Town center and church.
Photograph by R. Ceo.

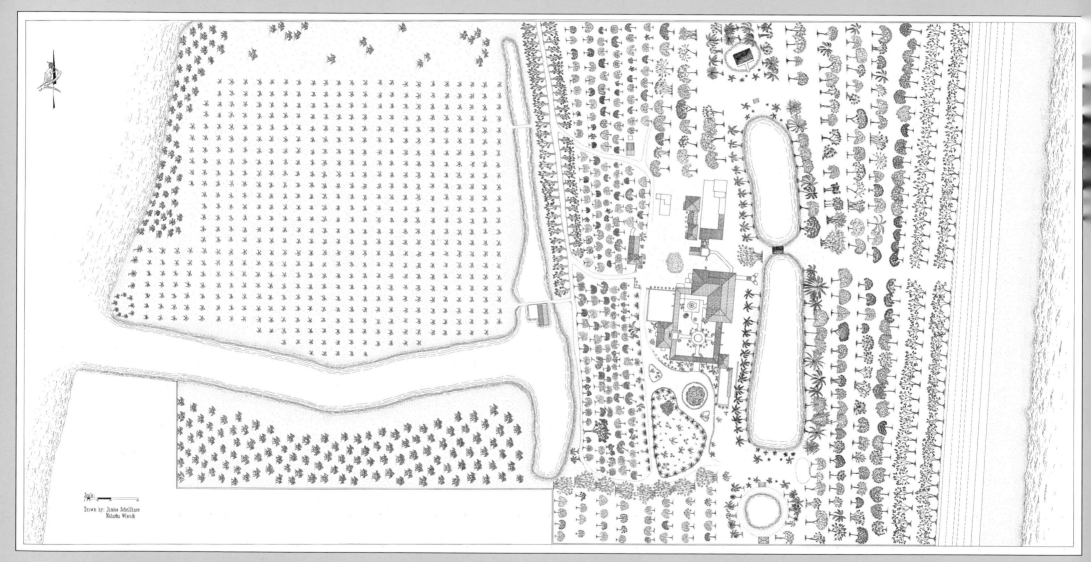

DRAWING BY: JANICE SHELLHASE, NATASHA WINNICK

55" X 36", HORIZONTAL FORMAT, INK ON MYLAR, 1993

Hugh Taylor Birch, a Chicago lawyer, acquired the oceanfront property that is now Hugh Taylor Birch State Park and Bonnet House in the late nineteenth century. By 1898, Birch had built a two-room frame cottage there.[1] When his daughter Helen married Frederic Clay Bartlett in January of 1919, Birch gave the couple a wedding gift of a thirty-five acre parcel of his three miles of land along the Atlantic Ocean. Soon the more architecturally ambitious Bonnet House, named for the lily of nearby Bonnet Slough, and designed by Frederic Bartlett, a painter and muralist, began to take form. Since Frederic and Helen were traveling, Hugh Taylor Birch supervised its construction.[2]

Door to courtyard.
Photograph by R. Ceo.

Jayne Rice in her account, *Bonnet House, Reflections of a Legacy*, describes the artistic career of Frederic Bartlett. He was an accomplished artist who designed the interior of Chicago's University Club, including its stained glass windows and "the ceiling panels of the Club's Michigan Room." In 1895 Bartlett had collaborated with the architect Howard Van Doren Shaw to produce "House in the Woods" in Geneva,

Wisconsin, for Bartlett's father Adolphus Clay Bartlett.[3] The house was built around a courtyard and Bartlett reproduced a diagram of it in his plan for Bonnet House. However, Geneva's winters were very different from the benevolence of the Florida climate, which permitted Bartlett to wrap loggias around the central courtyard and to open porches that overlooked the principal views. The character of the architecture is truly hybrid with Caribbean roots in the porches and fanciful exterior details, Mediterranean references in its courtyard diagram, and European, particularly German, elements derived from Bartlett's residence abroad, including his baroque ornamentation enlivening a doorway and the *wunderkammer* with its shell collection.

Bartlett had been inspired by Chicago's Columbian Exposition in 1893 to study at the Royal Academy in Munich. He then continued his studies "in Paris at the *Ecole Collin* for drawing, Aman-Jean's school for painting, and the *Academie Colarossi* for figure drawing," with later work in the studio of James McNeill Whistler.[4] By the time Bartlett designed Bonnet House, he had experienced European architecture and gardens directly. The architecture and landscape of Bonnet House provided Bartlett with an opportunity to integrate his interests

Pavilion and lagoon.
Photograph by R. Ceo.

in painterly composition with the issues presented by three-dimensional design to produce "not only the house of an artist but also an artistic house," as the home of his contemporary, the Swedish painter Carl Larsson, has been described.[5]

The size and location of the estate spanned a variety of topographic conditions. The New River Sound with the Florida East Coast Canal formed the estate's western edge, while the Bonnet Slough and the Atlantic Ocean lay to the east. The range of native plants, from coastal hardwood hammock to mangrove, seemed to invite experimentation with plant materials.

Six years after Helen Birch Bartlett's death in 1925, Frederic Bartlett married Evelyn Fortune Lilly.

The Bonnet House

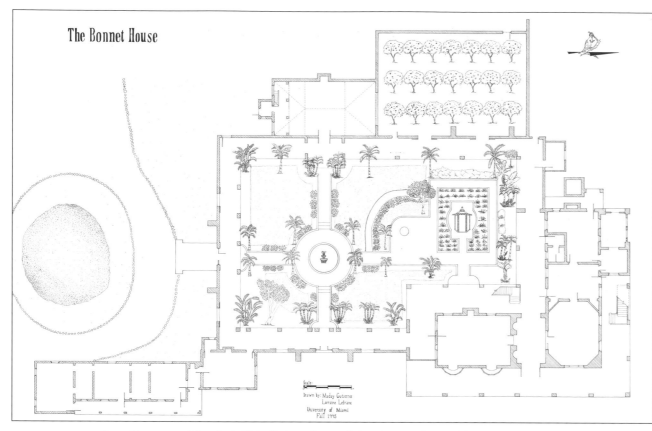

Bonnet House courtyard. Drawing by Maday Gutierrez, Lorraine Lefranc. 24" x 36", horizontal format, ink on mylar, 1995.

waterway to the east, while experimental fruit groves extended to the west. After the Army Corps of Engineers deposited fill from the dredging operation that created the Intracoastal Waterway in the late 1920s, the mangrove and buttonwood to the west of the house could no longer survive, so Bartlett developed a coconut plantation in their stead.[7]

The use of native materials as a context for exotics is a theme that links the architecture with the landscape of Bonnet House. Just as native limestone, seashells, and pine establish an architecture that is then highlighted with imported objects, the coastal hardwood hammock establishes a frame against which the exotic palms and fruits can be read. Today, its conservation of native conditions long lost to the rest of Fort Lauderdale may

She was also an artist, and the two continued to enhance Bonnet House. They created fanciful pavilions, one of which was the *wunderkammer* of the shell collection, another a tent-like structure next to the pond, and a third, the theater at the opposite end of the lagoon. They also built a stone fountain for the south allée.[6]

The Bartletts designed more of the landscape, creating gardens, each with a character that related to its adjacent architecture and its specific site. Within the entry sequence

that begins in a wooded allée, and then reaches a clearing, they heightened the contrast of dark and light with specific plant selections. An arid plant collection, for example, surrounds the outer gate in a bright clearing, while within the central courtyard, tropical specimens prevail. They brought whimsy to the construction of an aviary, relating it to the tropical theme of the court. Beyond the central court, the landscape alters to suit changing conditions. A broad lawn overlooks the

Coastal hammock walk east of the lagoon.
Photograph by R. Ceo.

Front elevation by Erika Albright and Jason Bush, 24" x 36", ink on mylar, 1995.

Courtyard section by Erika Albright and Jason Bush, 24" x 36", ink on mylar, 1995.

be one of the most important contributions that the Bonnet House offers. Evelyn Bartlett's commitment to the estate continued until her death in 1997. She was responsible for deeding the property in 1983 to the Florida Trust for Historic Preservation, an organization dedicated to the ongoing presence of Florida's history in contemporary life.

In addition to its historical significance, the skill demonstrated in the landscape and architecture here and the singular vision of designers whose palette included the grounds as well as the building, make this property a significant work of garden art.

–JL

Notes:

1. Pamela Euston, "'Big Boss' The Life and Times of Hugh Taylor Birch," unpublished paper for Dr. Paul S. George (Florida Atlantic University, April 24, 1989), 57.

2. Euston, 1989, 71-2.

3. Jayne Rice, *Reflections of a Legacy: The Bonnet House Story* (Fort Lauderdale: Bonnet House, 1989), 52.

4. Rice, 1989, 50.

5. Michael Snodin and Elisabet Stavenow-Hidemark, editors, *Carl and Karin Larsson: Creators of the Swedish Style* (New York: Bulfinch Press [1997] 1998), 95.

6. Rice, 1989, 93.

7. Rice, 1989, 82.

Lagoon and house looking southwest.
Photograph by R. Ceo.

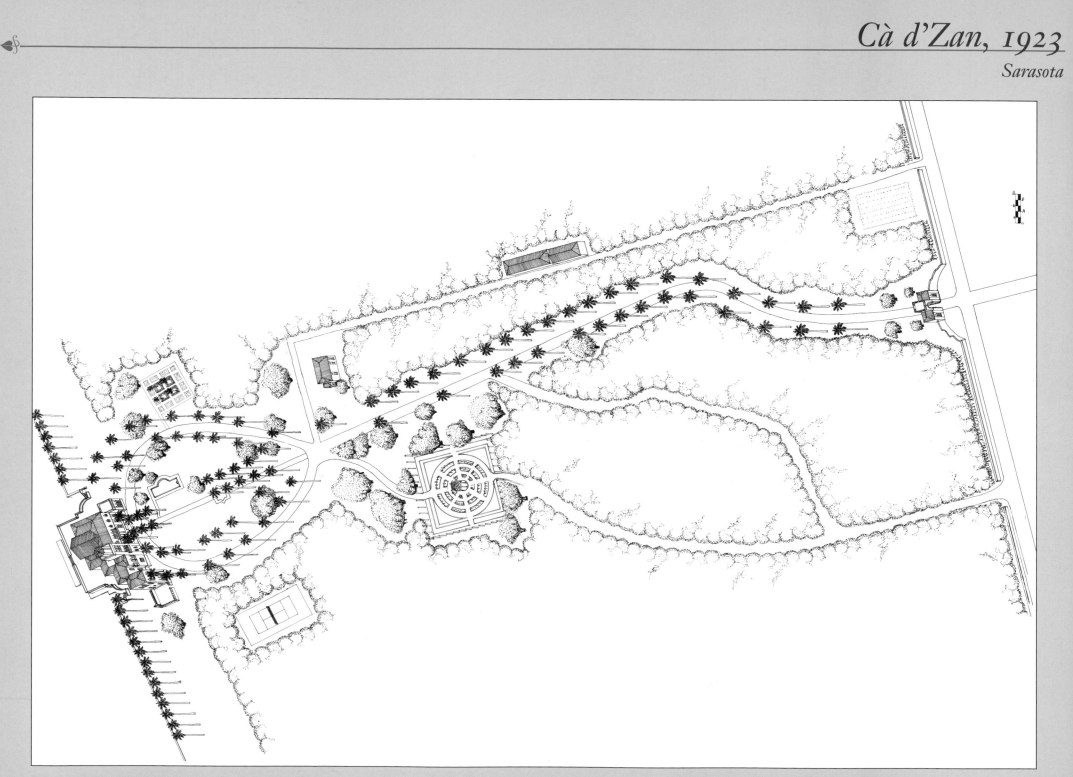

DRAWING BY: PATRICK CAMPBELL
24" X 36", VERTICAL FORMAT, INK ON MYLAR, 1992

Cà d'Zan is the product of a collaboration between a noted New York architect, Dwight James Baum, and his clients, John and Mable Ringling, who built the estate as their winter home. Mrs. Ringling took a particularly active role in the project while her husband was producing the circus' *Greatest Show on Earth*. Their European travels and love of Venice, in particular the Doge's Palace, inspired Mable Ringling to accumulate a folio of images of Venetian buildings. She began the project with architect, Thomas Martin. Casting further from Mrs Ringling's folio, Martin chose as a model Cà d'Oro, the fifteenth century Venetian palazzo, known for its gothic architecture and the gilt-work for which it was named. Martin had come to the attention of the Ringlings

Entrance walk.
Cà d'Zan Collection.

through his work with French garden designer and restorationist, Achille Duchêne, on Mrs. Potter Palmer's estate, The Oaks, at Osprey, just south of Sarasota. Mr. and Mrs. Ringling had admired The Oaks and began with Martin the process of

designing an estate for their own thirty-eight acres. But after a year, the project was suspended, not to be revived until Baum took it on again in 1923.[1]

Baum was a graduate of the architecture school at Syracuse University where he later collaborated with John Russell Pope to design the Georgian style Hendricks Memorial Chapel. His education had prepared him for the study and analysis necessary to produce buildings in a variety of styles, so he was responsive to the Ringlings' interest in the architecture of Venice and Martin's earlier inspiration of the association with Cà d'Oro. Beyond his work at Cà d'Zan, Baum also designed the Sarasota County Courthouse and the El Vernona Hotel, a building that Michael McDonough, an architectural historian and designer in Sarasota, considers "particularly effective in establishing the new look of Sarasota."[2]

McDonough credits John Ringling with focusing first on the Mediterranean architecture that became characteristic of Sarasota, not only in his own home, but in the subdivisions and hotels that he was developing locally. From the California Building at the World's Columbian Exposition of 1893, and the Fair's Street of Cairo exhibit, McDonough tracks the growing popularity of Mediterranean themes in amusement parks,

movies and movie theatres of the 1920s:

By the mid 1920s, most Americans had strong, positive associations with the architectural styles of the Mediterranean basin since they had seen them almost exclusively in entertainment, recreation, and travel environments. Like movie producers, Sarasota real estate salesmen sold atmosphere and romance. Illusion was Sarasota's main staple. Here, for the price of a modest down payment, the visitor from a small Northern town could buy a piece of a grand Mediterranean fantasy.[3]

Cà d'Zan was the apotheosis of the ideas Ringling was selling in his subdivisions and hotels. The process of design for the lavish Cà d'Zan was much published in its own era and is

Postcard showing aerial view of mansion.
Rocco Ceo Collection.

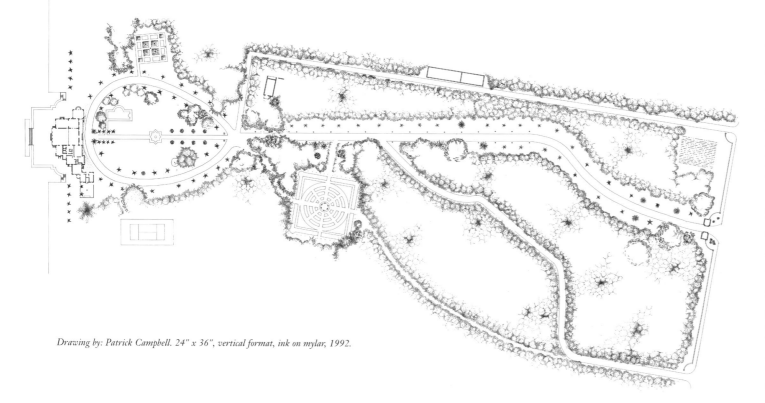

Drawing by: Patrick Campbell. 24" x 36", vertical format, ink on mylar, 1992.

Views from the 1920s and 30s profile the villa against a dense hammock. Closer examination of the photos reveals the presence of the pines and palmettos that normally composed the plant communities of the Gulf shore coastline. Roger Franklin Sears wrote about Cà d'Zan for the British magazine *Country Life* in October of 1927, and noted that "one approaches the house from a long drive shaded by palms on either side circling up to the house and to the main entrance." The drama of approaching Cà d'Zan through a dense wooded hammock would have made the sight of its great 200-foot frontage along Sarasota Bay seem all the more vast, if not like an outpost.

Plantings within the garden have been attributed to Mable Ringling, who, when the workmen cleared palmetto and muck to prepare for the gardens and mansion, was said to "wade along with them in high boots, pistol in hand, on

well documented in James T. Maher's book, *The Twilight of Splendor: Chronicles of the Age of American Palaces*. So much about the house is known in such detail that discussion of it tends to obscure the role of the gardens within the overall composition. However, the gardens merit more thorough analysis. Although Mable Ringling's rose garden often dominates the literature, the larger garden is also important, including the gardens shaped as museum halls for the Ringlings' sculpture collection. Within these garden rooms, art objects were placed in settings that contrasted the refined pieces of sculpture with exotic plants and native scrub. Further study may illuminate the thinking behind the creation of these and other gardens on the estate.

Marble statues and yaupon plants (Ilex vomitoria) along path to rose garden.
Photograph by R. Ceo.

Pool flanking automobile entrance.
Postcard, Rocco Ceo Collection.

Postcard, Rocco Ceo Collection.

the alert for snakes."[4] Although the house is linked with Venice proper, the description of Mable in the brush sounds more like what the Venetians might have encountered when they left the city to build the villas of the Veneto, where they too carved urbane estates out of rough countryside. While Cà d'Zan looks to the Doges' Palace of Venice for its model, the

Ringlings' estate was a rural landscape, yet the largesse of its gestures suggested a presence that could command a future city. Now that the wilderness beyond the estate has become developed, the urbanity of the great axis of Cà d'Zan, the foreground of its formal garden rooms, and the civic expanse of its waterfront vista is perhaps even more effective today.

–JL

Fountain surrounded by banyan trees.
Cà d'Zan Collection.

Notes:

1. James T. Maher, *The Twilight of Splendor* (Boston and Toronto: Little, Brown and Company, 1975), 106-112.

2. Michael McDonough, "Selling Sarasota: Architecture and Propaganda in a 1920s BoomTown", *Florida Theme Issue: The Journal of the Decorative and Propaganda Arts 1875-1945*, 23 (1998): 30.

3. McDonough, 1998, 17.

4. "Mable and Edith are the Best Known of the Ringlings," *St. Petersburg Times*, January 30, 1966, 4.

Rose garden and gazebo.
Photograph by R. Ceo.

WILLIAM LYMAN PHILLIPS

Joanna Lombard

The Phillips contribution to the landscape of Florida is almost immeasurable. William Lyman Phillips appreciated native materials and was judicious in his introduction of exotics. The compositional principles that directed his work came from an excellent education, years of travel and observation, and exceptional abilities that overlap architecture and engineering. From the grand gesture of the axis of Fairchild Tropical Garden's Overlook, in which Vincent Scully recognized the same driving force that inspired Andre LeNotre at Versailles, to the delicate carving of a singular path through the mangrove to the sea at Matheson Hammock, Phillips relied on ordering principles to arrange native materials to great effect.

The fundamental principles that inspired Phillips are rooted in the practice and writings of Frederick Law Olmsted, America's premier landscape architect of the nineteenth century. Olmsted and his firm in Brookline, Massachusetts, completed extensive projects across the United States; his ideas extended to a new generation, when Charles Eliot, an Olmsted partner, began to argue for a professional program in landscape architecture at Harvard University. Eliot's premature death inspired his father Charles W. Eliot, then president of Harvard University, to found Harvard's landscape program in the fall of 1900 and, in 1903, to award the Charles Eliot Professorship to Frederick Law Olmsted, Jr.[1]

A review of the writings of Eliot and Olmsted, as well as the curriculum at Harvard in those early years reveals a unified philosophy that engendered several powerful precepts for the profession. First, one finds consensus that the purpose of landscape architecture lay in the "art of arranging land and landscape for human use, convenience, and enjoyment."[2] Those words reappear almost precisely on the first page of William Lyman Phillips' notebook from Professor James Sturgis Prey's introductory course, Landscape Architecture I, offered at Harvard in the fall of 1908. Second, Olmsted and Eliot believed that landscape architects hold the professional responsibility for what Eliot called "the main lines" of the project.[3] And finally they believed in the formal principle of unity, in which "the site, the scene, the landscape," and the buildings should be studied as one composition.[4]

Unity as an overarching idea was widely held as a goal in design. In Eliot's era, Andrew Jackson Downing, an important nineteenth-century writer on the American landscape, said that "Unity, *or the production of a whole*, is a leading principle of the highest importance."[5] This dedication to unity was thought to produce a clear image of a landscape in those who experienced it directly. Olmsted, in his "Description of a Plan for the Improvement of the Central Park, 'Greensward,' 1858, declared that "The idea of the park itself should always be uppermost in the mind of the beholder."[6] William Lyman Phillips restates this idea in his own class notes, writing that "the goal of landscape architecture is a complex, but unified impression."[7]

Upon his graduation from the landscape program in 1910, Phillips worked in Montreal on the design of several parks. Then in 1911, he joined Olmsted Brothers as an assistant with responsibility for site work on the Boston Common, as well as for contracts and specifications. He took a leave from the firm in 1913, and after four months of independent European travel, Phillips was awarded the position of landscape architect, responsible for "the design and construction of the new town of Balboa," for the Isthmian Canal Commission where he lived on site for the next sixteen months.[8]

Matheson Hammock Park trail.
Photograph by R. Ceo.

When Phillips returned to Cambridge in the winter of 1914, he found very little work, although he pursued leads for positions around the country. For the next several years Phillips moved around the U.S. until he landed at Camp Bragg, South Carolina in 1919 and began working on layouts for Army establishments. Over the next five years Phillips successively practiced in Brookline, spent a year based in Paris where he worked on American military cemeteries, continued his travels in Europe and the U.S., and then finally settled on the west coast of Florida where he planned a new town on the island of Boca Grande, to be developed by a chemical

Bridge at Greynolds Park.
Photograph by R. Ceo.

Although his peers recognized the high quality of Phillips' work throughout his life, Florida's isolation so far south contributed to his obscurity from the national perspective. Phillips commented on the circumstance, but felt that Florida had become his palette and he was reluctant to change his situation. Within Florida, however, his landscapes were highly visible and his public parks at Crandon, Greynolds, and Matheson Hammock, as well as his outstanding accomplishment in the design and construction of Fairchild Tropical Garden, have defined Florida for generations of residents and their visitors.

company. Phillips moved to Lake Wales, Florida, in 1925, when the company decided to abandon real estate development. Phillips renewed his association with Olmsted Brothers and began work on Mountain Lake Sanctuary with Frederick Law Olmsted, Jr., who had become the firm's senior partner.

Phillips' collaboration with Olmsted continued for the rest of Olmsted's life and was the basis for Phillips' long career in Florida where he designed private, public, commercial, and institutional landscapes until his death on October eighteenth, 1966. The range of Phillips' work in Miami alone is broad. He produced institutional landscapes, such as the University of Miami; cemeteries, including Woodlawn and Inman; private clubs, including the Indian Creek County Club and the Biscayne Bay Yacht Club; numerous roadways and bridges, including The Venetian and Rickenbacker Causeways, as well as hundreds of private residences and businesses. In northern Florida his major works included a Riverfront Promenade for St. Augustine, further south, Mountain Lake Sanctuary in Lake Wales, Highland Hammock Park in Sebring, McKee Jungle Gardens in Vero Beach, and at the southern tip of the peninsula, the Overseas Highway to the Keys.

Notes:

1. James Sturgis Pray, "The Department of Landscape Architecture in Harvard University," *Landscape Architecture*, I, no. 2 (January 1911): 54-56.

2. Charles W. Eliot, *Charles Eliot, Landscape Architect* (Boston and New York: Houghton and Mifflin Company, 1902), 274.

3. Ibid., 367.

4. Ibid., 366.

5. Andrew Jackson Downing, *A Treatise on the Theory and Practice of Landscape Gardening* (New York: A.O. Moore & Co [1841] 1859), 64.

6. Frederick Law Olmsted, Sr., *Forty Years of Landscape Architecture: Central Park*, eds. Frederick Law Olmsted, Jr. and Theodora Kimball (1928; reprint, Cambridge, Massachusetts and London England, The M.I.T. Press, 1973), 222.

7. Notes by William Lyman Phillips, 1908, File 23-5, William Lyman Phillips Papers, Research Center, Historical Museum of Southern Florida, Miami, Florida.

8. Phillips to Waugh, 30 October 1915, File 14-5, William Lyman Phillips Papers, Research Center, Historical Museum of Southern Florida, Miami, Florida.

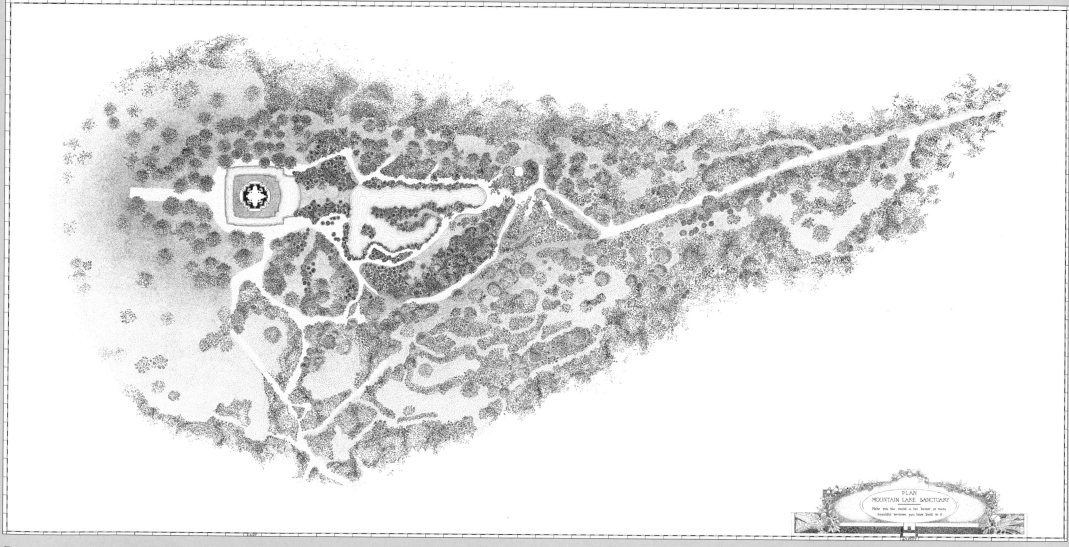

PLAN
MOUNTAIN LAKE SANCTUARY

Make you the world a bit better or more
beautiful because you have lived in it

DRAWING BY: RUTH DURANT, PATRICK SZUTAR
31" X 60", HORIZONTAL FORMAT, INK ON MYLAR, 1993

Edward Bok, editor of *The Ladies' Home Journal*, began planning the Sanctuary at Mountain Lake in 1922. An immigrant from the Netherlands, Bok was also widely known for his Pulitzer Prize winning autobiography, *The Americanization of Edward Bok*, published in 1921. His editorship at the *Journal* was characterized by an interest in significant issues, including women's suffrage and environmental concerns. Among these was an effort to halt the carnage of Florida's native birds by asking *Journal* readers to stop wearing the feathers of these endangered species.

In 1929, Bok formally dedicated the Sanctuary and its carillon tower to the American people with the hope of preserving some of Florida's natural beauty in its flora and fauna. The Sanctuary occupies 157 acres on the wooded, northern slope of Iron Mountain, the only such hill in central Florida. Located just outside Fred Ruth's 2000 acres of citrus groves and his resort community of 500 acres called the Mountain Lake Colony, Bok's Sanctuary was to be a landscape for his own use and pleasure, ". . . open and accessible to his friends and neighbors of the Mountain Lake Colony."[1] Ruth had hired the leading landscape architecture firm in the country, Olmsted Brothers of Brookline, to design the colony, and Bok chose Olmsted to design the Sanctuary as well. William Lyman Phillips is regarded as the chief project designer, since he represented Olmsted Bothers in Lake Wales from the Sanctuary's inception in 1924 through its completion in 1931. Phillips collaborated with Frederick Law Olmsted, Jr., on the design and construction of the Sanctuary, directed all of the site work, and designed a number of gardens for homeowners in Mountain Lake Colony.

Frederick Law Olmsted, Jr. wrote to Edward Bok while traveling by train on the fourth of July, 1922, to outline his design concept. Olmsted described a wooded climb across the hillside with several lookout points along the way. The climb would culminate in a plateau, selectively cleared and planted to frame views of the panoramic vistas at the top. Olmsted detailed the layout in terms that captivated Bok and revealed Olmsted's mastery of the intricacies

of his art and craft. He proposed that the approach by road should originate in a "flattish, shady grove for parking," from which the visitor would advance toward the eastern entrance to discover "the glorious western view" by "having it burst upon him."[2] The parking grove was to be surrounded by orange groves, and the home sites of the Mountain Lake Colony beyond. Olmsted pictured a variegated wood, beginning with the native pine landscape, to which he suggested adding live oaks, laurel oaks, and other broad-leaved evergreens.

The landscape architect considered the parking grove "a sort of antechamber to the Sanctuary."[3] The actual Sanctuary entrance would be:

a rather narrow passage, at least one or two hundred feet in length, rising gently through a dense wood, completely overarched by trees and flanked on either hand by a seemingly

Live oak walk.
Photograph by R. Ceo.

impenetrable thicket of under-growth. It should be just long enough and just sufficiently indirect in its easy curvature for one to shake off his impressions of the road and of the automobiles and of the orange groves as roadside companions, and to feel that he is penetrating into something different.[4]

"A rapid, but not arduous, rise" was to cross the hill diagonally toward the northwest. Along the rise, "thickets would begin to clear" and one "would merge into patches of low bushy growth over which the eye would range." Olmsted wanted a thicket similar to the "bushy pastures studded with junipers, [and] blueberries" in New England, that would give way to "distant views, across the pine ridges to Lake Pierce."

The climb would continue through trees and evergreen shrubs, such as wax myrtle, with fern and floral ground covers until it reached a small plateau that Olmsted planned to enlarge to create a level plane from which a new crest would ascend. On the first plateau he meant to recreate the hammock typically found along the shoreline between mangrove and pineland. This hammock scenery "would be the heart of the Sanctuary, completely self-contained and shut off from the rest of the world, — a little sunlit forest glade surrounded by dense shadow." Next he left a "narrow belt of undergrowth" and then laid out:

an open grove of Live Oaks and Long Leaf Pine, not over forty or fifty feet wide east and west but a couple of hundred yards long north and south, nearly level and backed on the east by the dense "hammock" growth much as that growth backs the beach of many a Florida lake. On the west the ground would drop away, more precipitously for the first ten or fifteen feet of drop than it does at present, as precipitously indeed as would seem at all natural in this sandy soil.[5]

Olmsted described to Bok the devices he was depending upon to enhance the drama of the climb sequence, which included shrouding views to focus the visitor's attention on the climactic falling away of the foreground, and framing the distant view with live oaks and pines.

From the height of the Sanctuary, the return trip would amble along the uppermost plateau with a hollow to its south and "a winding dumbbell-shaped pond, perhaps a hundred and fifty feet long, with characteristic water-side vegetation and likely to become a happy haunt of the birds." Olmsted also suggested that a caretaker's cottage might become a gate-lodge between the parking grove and the Sanctuary. The Boks responded "most favorably" adding only a concern about how the pond might be constructed, and a general query regarding costs.[6]

The project rapidly moved forward, so that by 1931 Olmsted was writing to Mrs. Bok discussing the "removal of surplus plants."[7] At this point he was also concerned about maintaining the proper heights of plant materials to preserve the central idea of the surprising vista at the conclusion of the climb. He explained that if the shrubs below the trees grew too tall, one "might look through the woods and out the other side of them with a serious loss of mystery and seclusion."[8]

Tower and reflecting pool.
Photograph by R. Ceo.

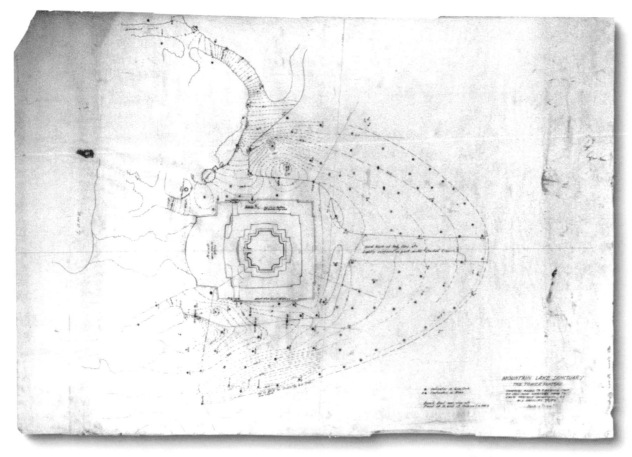

After completing Olmsted's initial landscape design, Bok engaged the Philadelphia architect, Milton B. Medary, to design and build the carillon tower. The firm of Zantzinger, Borie and Medary were well regarded for their work on many important institutional buildings, including the Department of Justice Building in Washington (1931-5), the Philadelphia Museum of Art (1926-28), buildings at Princeton and Yale, as well as the Burton-Judson Courts at the University of Chicago (1929-31) where Beatrix

Farrand was the landscape architect.

The siting of the Medary tower was the responsibility of Olmsted Brothers and Phillips' drawings place the tower within a moat connecting the original pond to a new pond aligned with the northerly axis of the new tower. From the green around the tower, a path down the hill toward the east was also built leading to new parking for residents and guests of the Colony. The twenty-story tower and garden were dedicated by

President Coolidge in 1929. At the ceremony, Bok said he

> *wanted to present to the American people for visitation . . . a spot which would reach out in its beauty through the plantings, through the flowers, through the birds, through the superbly beautiful architecture of the Tower, through the music of the bells, to the people and fill their souls with the quiet, the repose, the influence of the beautiful, as they could see and enjoy it in the Sanctuary and the Tower.[9]*

Because the climb through the Sanctuary ascent had been conceived with a limited number of visitors in mind — Bok, his friends and the residents and visitors of Mountain Lake Colony — the large crowds arriving for carillon concerts threatened some aspects of the landscape. While the open areas proved to be large enough for the unanticipated number of visitors, the intricacies of the ascent suffered from overuse. By 1956, the Bok family and the Olmsted office began to consider how the Sanctuary might better accommodate the growing numbers of visitors and remain true to its original contemplative intent.

Phillips, in association with the Olmsted office, prepared a report on the Sanctuary in 1956 which extended the original concept of "contrast between closed and open scenery" to a new scale that would make an "addition of more closed units — the reflection view, the Resurrection Garden — and of more open passages — the Tower grove and the panoramic views to the east, south and west."[10] The report noted that the tower now "dominated the composition," not only in its commanding figure at the top of Iron Mountain, but also:

in public understanding. For unfortunately the words "Bok Tower" were considered by makers of road signs and writers of press notices to be preferable to any longer and more comprehensive designations, and this title has become so universally used that to mention the Mountain Lake Sanctuary is ordinarily to utter an enigma. The Tower has the fame, the carillon concerts are what one has to attend.

Still, the larger landscape was Phillips' concern, as it had been for Bok, and Phillips felt the Sanctuary must not be sacrificed to the skewed priorities of a commercialized world. He also recognized its power over visitors, a new multitude perhaps:

Yet the Sanctuary as a whole is still valid in the concept of its founder. It is the part of the world that he left more beautiful than he found it. Regardless of the motives by which people are drawn there, the Sanctuary, once entered, affects the senses of the visitor gratefully, creates a poetic mood, induces feelings of reverence, stirs the mind to rapt admiration. Here voices are hushed as in a church, and decency for the moment takes possession of the vulgar.

A more striking example of the power of beauty could hardly be found, better proof that her beauty exists could not be asked for.[11]

Phillips urged Judge Curtis Bok, the founder's son, to address accruing problems with maintenance, as well as the management of visitors and concluded the Olmsted report of 1956 with a strong appeal to Judge Bok to understand the importance of planning to protect "this complex of plant life existing under partly artificial conditions, always changing, tending to evolve always into something different from what we see."[12] Unfortunately, this report seems to have provoked Judge Bok, whose reactions and intentions were the subject of several subsequent letters between Phillips and the Olmsted office in Brookline.

Frederick Law Olmsted, Jr. died on Christmas day of 1957, and the following spring Phillips wondered whether "F.L.O., confronted by the problem of providing a setting for a carillon, visited by hundreds of people at a time, would have come up with what we see now, speaking more especially of the old Sanctuary area. The Tower had been completed, the moat and reflection pool made, when E. Bok decided to open the place to the public."[13] Phillips, who had spent the past thirty years connected to the Sanctuary, pondered how best to accommodate the gardens' numerous visitors and still preserve what he called the place where he felt "more

> *"…the Sanctuary, once entered, affects the senses of the visitor gratefully, creates a poetic mood, induces feelings of reverence, stirs the mind to rapt admiration."*
> – William Lyman Phillips

Palms and azaleas in springtime.
Photograph by Michael L. Carlebach.

73

satisfaction of being than in any other piece of humanized ground."[14]

By May of 1958, Judge Curtis Bok agreed to increase maintenance of the paths and thickets to preserve Olmsted's original principle of contrast between open and closed spaces, while Phillips agreed that magnolias could be introduced along the western edge in order to build new areas of interest that would not conflict with the original intent of the design.

While landscape architecture of the 1950s was changing direction and the modern garden was moving closer to modern painting, Olmsted and Phillips continued to rely on formal organization and structure to provide the essential bones of the body of design. They confirmed the principle of unity, the first Frederick Law Olmsted's view that a landscape design should enable people to form an idea of a place that would stay with them. And finally, they lived the role of the landscape architect that Charles Eliot advocated in which the landscape architect set the main lines of the project. Architects, engineers, horticulturists, and many others participated in creating the Sanctuary, but Olmsted and Phillips were fundamentally responsible for the character that continues to make the Sanctuary a memorable landscape.

–JL

Tower photographed by William Lyman Phillips.
Historical Museum of Southern Florida.

Notes:

1. "The Mountain Lake Sanctuary, Mountain Lake, Florida: A Report," Olmsted Brothers, Landscape Architects, Brookline, Massachusetts and William Lyman Phillips, Landscape Architect, North Miami, Florida, 2 July 1956, File 8-4, William Lyman Phillips Papers, Research Center, Historical Museum of Southern Florida, Miami, Florida.

2. Olmsted to Bok, 7 July 1922, File 7-22, William Lyman Phillips Papers, Research Center, Historical Museum of Southern Florida, Miami, Florida.

3. Ibid.

4. Ibid.

5. Ibid.

6. Bok to Olmsted, 10 July 1922, File 7-22, William Lyman Phillips Papers, Research Center, Historical Museum of Southern Florida, Miami, Florida.

7. Olmsted to Bok, 28 March 1931, File 7-22, William Lyman Phillips Papers, Research Center, Historical Museum of Southern Florida, Miami, Florida.

8. Ibid.

9. Edward W. Bok, "A Personal Foreword," *The Sanctuary and Singing Tower* (Mountain Lake, Florida: The American Foundation Incorporated, 1929).

10. "The Mountain Lake Sanctuary, Mountain Lake, Florida: A Report," Olmsted Brothers, Landscape Architects, Brookline, Massachusetts and William Lyman Phillips, Landscape Architect, North Miami, Florida, 2 July 1956, File 8-4, William Lyman Phillips Papers, Research Center, Historical Museum of Southern Florida, Miami, Florida.

11. Ibid.

12. Ibid.

13. Phillips to Marquis and Whiting, 14 April 1958, File 5-7, William Lyman Phillips Papers, Research Center, Historical Museum of Southern Florida, Miami, Florida.

14. Phillips to Marquis, 12 April 1958, Files 5-7, William Lyman Phillips Papers, Research Center, Historical Museum of Southern Florida, Miami, Florida.

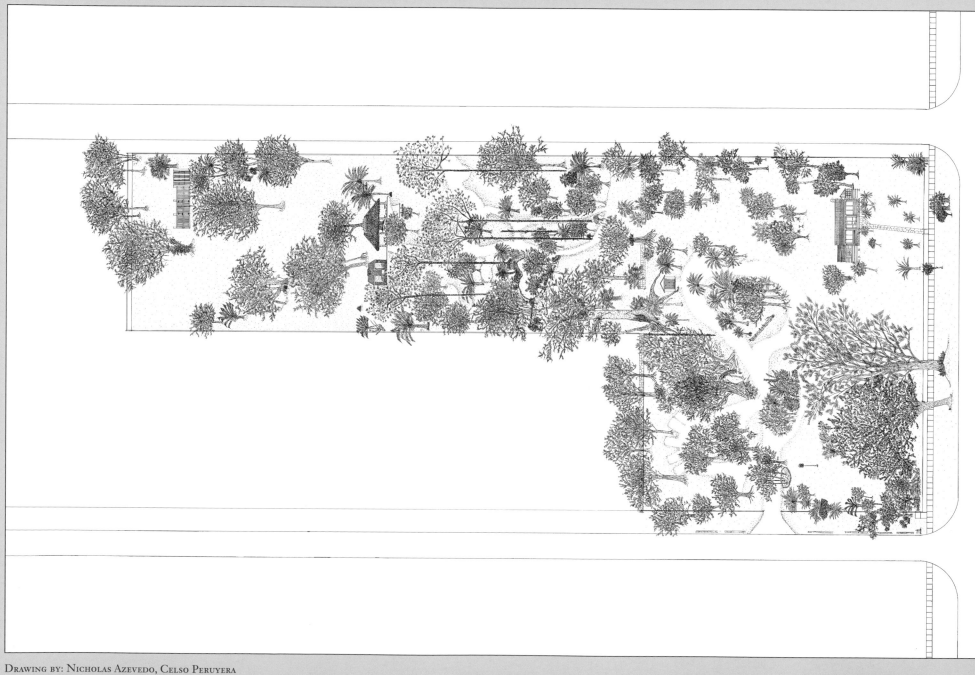

DRAWING BY: NICHOLAS AZEVEDO, CELSO PERUYERA
24" X 36", VERTICAL FORMAT, INK ON MYLAR, 1995

The grounds of the "Doc" Thomas House have evolved over the years from three acres of pineland around a homestead to a wonderful collection of native garden plots that document subtle differences in South Florida's plant communities. "Doc" was Arden Hayes Thomas, a pharmacist who founded the OK Drug Store and OK Feed Store in Dade County. When he moved to Dade County in the

House and front grounds.
Photograph by R. Ceo.

1920s, Thomas became, like many before him, enchanted with the area and its unique landscape and he followed the lead of many early homesteaders by clearing the land around the house he soon built. The clearings opened the house to the breezes and kept vegetation off the rot-sensitive wood used in construction. Exotic plants such as crotons or fishtail palms were added for color or focus outside porches or along paths. Acquaintances and friends, including David Fairchild, often made gifts of plants and contributed to the diversity of plants found on the site.

"Doc" Thomas donated the house to the Tropical Audubon Society in 1974, a year before his death. The only restriction put on the gift was that the building and grounds be preserved and used for environmental education. The current garden is a product of preservation of important non-native species of the original homestead, the removal of most of the invasive plants, and the design and planting of new native demonstration gardens by members of the Tropical Audubon Society.

The garden is divided roughly into two plots with the northern plot around the house consisting of pineland and hammock and the southern half of the site containing the Brookfield Hammock and Key's native plantings. George Gann, who intended to help illustrate the geographic diversity of South Florida by identifying different types of hammocks and pineland communities, prepared the restoration plan for the northeast portion of the property. Gann laid out a plan for sixteen native plant communities of which eight represent hammocks and hammock edges and eight represent pinelands and pineland edges. The extensive Keys habitat on the southern half of the site is largely the effort of David Lysinger who has acquired, catalogued, and planted many species here including the threatened Semapore cactus, *Opuntia spinosissima*.

Semapore cactus in Keys habitat garden.
Photograph by R. Ceo.

76

Detail of drawing showing pineland, chickee and outbuilding.

The importance of the garden lies not only in its collection of threatened or endangered plants but in the habitat it creates for birds and butterflies. In this way the garden serves to demonstrate the importance of the symbiotic relationship between the landscape and the fauna it helps preserve and the garden also acts as an urban viewing locale for bird and butterfly enthusiasts.

The house was built in 1931. It was designed by Robert Fitch Smith, one of the first professors in architecture at the University of Miami. Built of wide tidewater cypress siding and Dade-County pine, the house is a rare example of an Art Deco

Southern portion of property.
Photograph by R. Ceo.

Silver palm.
Photograph by R. Ceo.

The subtle native landscape and carefully crafted house form a partnership that parallels the original owner's intentions for the site. The demonstration gardens are well identified and allow visitors to learn more about xeriscape landscape principles. The building and garden comprise one of the last remaining sites that still offers a sensitive model for how building and landscape should coexist in a native landscape.

–RJC

Trail through pineland.
Photograph by R. Ceo.

design in wood. The modest size and hidden siting of the house mask the craft that lies within its interior. The main room reveals one of the finest wood floors in South Florida. It is made of random-width oak separated by walnut strips and accented with mahogany pegs. This large living space is edged on the south by a window seat and on the west end of the room, a large keystone and oolitic rock fireplace perfectly anchors the space, in its detail and proportion.

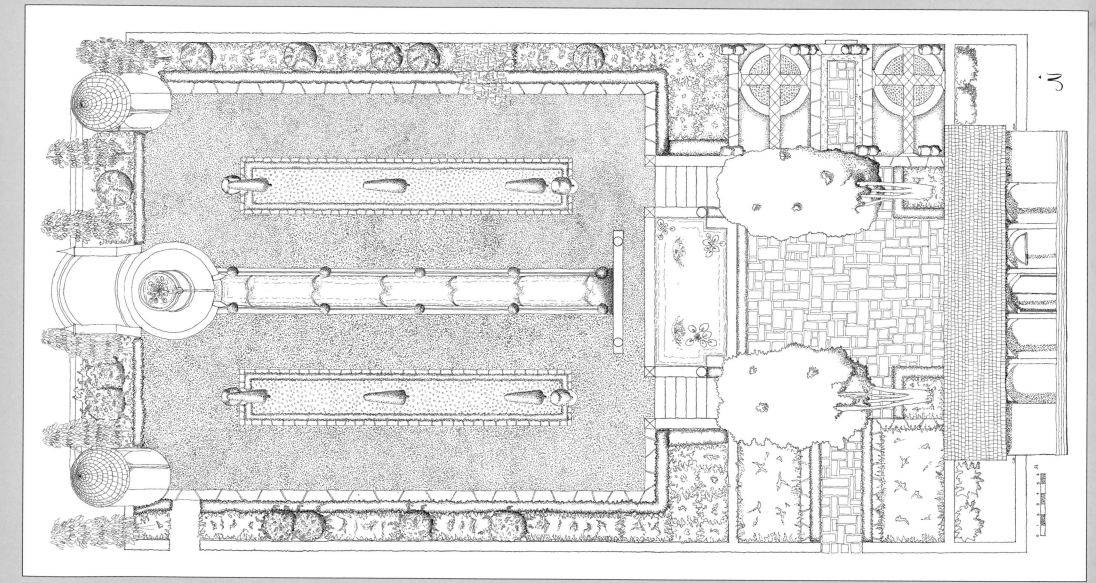

DRAWING BY: CLAUDIA BANCALARI, MORELLA MIGLIORELLI
18 ¼" X 30", VERTICAL FORMAT, INK ON MYLAR, 1992

Reflecting pool.
Photograph by R. Ceo.

On January 22, 1931 Nellie Cluett established the Cluett Memorial Garden in memory of her parents, George Bywater Cluett and his wife Amanda R. Cluett, and in doing so memorialized forty-two years of her family's involvement with Palm Beach's Episcopal Church of Bethesda-by-the-Sea.

The small garden is nestled behind the stately mass of this, the third Episcopal church of the community, at the rear of a city block. Its construction followed a building campaign begun in 1889 to provide a place of worship for a handful of residents settled along the banks of Lake Worth, which predated Palm Beach. With the building of the railroad by Henry Flagler, and the resultant increase in the population of winter visitors to his new hotel, the Royal Poinciana, Palm Beach was born and with it the need for a larger church. The new building was constructed by John H. Troy of New York. Impressive in scale and in detail with its high campanile and Moorish style, it served nobly for thirty-one years before giving way to the present building.

Between 1922 and 1926, the parish built its third church closer to the Atlantic Ocean, guided by the vision of Canon Russell, a man of lofty ideals and grand dreams. With it, Russell meant to commemorate the landing of Ponce De Leon on the Florida Coast in 1513. The church was designed by the architects Hiss and Weeks of New York in the style of Leon Cathedral in Spain. Though this was to be a modest place of worship on the banks of a lake, its form would allude to the grand event of the discovery of the New World. The theme of water is present in thoughtful details throughout the church, including stained glass windows that illustrate biblical accounts of events that took place at sea. But it is most powerfully expressed in the memorial gardens.

The healing properties of water and its capacity for transforming and redeeming are orchestrated in the Cluett garden, which measures only about 100' x 175'. Through the carefully orchestrated axis aligned through a fountain, reflecting pool, and a water channel, one moves against the direction of water that flows around the base of the channel before ascending stairs to an upper terrace called the Color Garden.

Postcard, Rocco Ceo Collection.

Reflecting pool with fountain at far end.
Postcard, Rocco Ceo Collection.

in the channel along its edge or the cup at your table. Including a place for conversation and refreshment in these gardens reminds us that a memorial need not be only for solemn reflection and melancholy. Located at the base of the Color Garden and closest to the garden's entrance, the Tea Garden was a setting for gatherings, with a well-outfitted kitchen and service rooms to accommodate outdoor events in the adjacent Normandy style building. Standing within the Tea Garden, because it lies below the Color Garden, one is put on eye level with the waterline of the reflecting pool, visible through an opening in the wall above the channel. The water from

Accompanied by the sound of the water, the Color Garden was meant as a place of solitude, contemplation and meditation, sheltered from the outside world. In the Color Garden one can

Della Robbia relief in the Tea Garden.
Photograph by R. Ceo.

"sit in one of the corner gazebos" and watch the "great-sailed Florida clouds go by" or "listen to the gentle splashing of water or the exuberant song of a mockingbird." A long reflecting pool connecting the fountain at the far end with the channel toward the teahouse divides the Color Garden's terrace of flower beds, each marked with boxwood hedges in the shape of a cross. The Color Garden is a place of pink and yellow hibiscus and the long creamy trumpets of datura, a place of visual beauty and constant change.

By contrast the Tea Garden is a place of interaction and socializing, where water was contained either

Turf bridge over reflecting pool.
Photograph by R. Ceo.

Drawing detail showing front entrance of garden.

the reflecting pool, like the tea we enjoy in this space, has a restorative quality, mixing both sacred and profane messages in one space with incredible ease and discipline.

The garden is remarkably well detailed and sensitively geared to the senses. With flowers that bloom in succession through most of the year and the constant sound of fountains and falling water we are reminded of the inevitable march of time. It is a memorial garden that is at once specific and universal.

–RJC

Postcard, Rocco Ceo Collection.

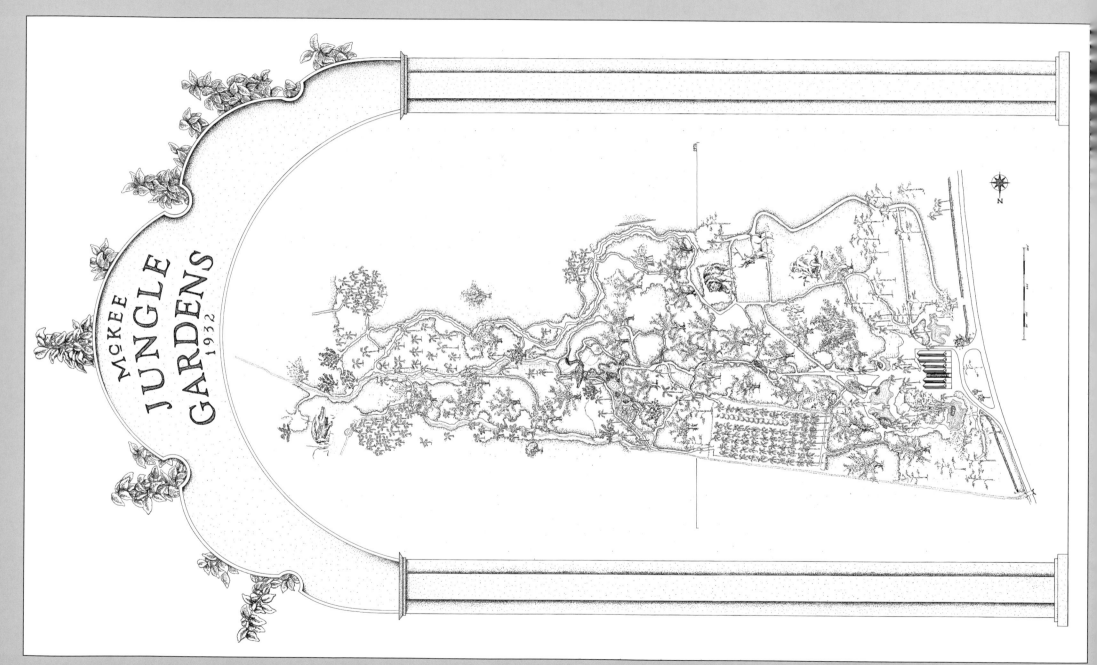

McKEE JUNGLE GARDENS 1932

DRAWING BY: RUTH DURANT, IVETTE GATELL, NICOLE RENEE HENRY, ARTHUR INFELD
36" x 48", VERTICAL FORMAT, INK ON MYLAR, 1994

McKee Jungle Gardens, like most great gardens, is the outcome of the labors of dedicated enthusiasts and skillful professionals who appreciated the site's natural beauty and identified opportunities for design. The Jungle Gardens grew out of the holdings of the McKee-Sexton Land Company which had been established in the 1920s. By the time Arthur G. McKee and Waldo E. Sexton opened the eighty-acre tract as McKee Jungle Gardens in 1932, they had engaged a powerful group of professionals. William Lyman Phillips was the consulting landscape architect, based in Miami. On site, landscape architect Winton H. Reinsmith, a former associate of Phillips from the Olmsted Brothers office, directed the work, with the assistance of Jens Hansen, the landscape superintendent.

Reinsmith told Phillips that the name McKee was attached only with "Mr. McKee's reluctant acquiescence," after persistent pressure from Sexton.[1] In July of 1930 Reinsmith was working toward opening day and recounted for Phillips the visits of plant experts who had ambitious goals for the Gardens' collections. The challenge of moving notable material into the garden, however, was at the forefront of his thinking, and Reinsmith recounted the process of relocating:

a 35 foot Coconut Palm from town onto the peninsula near the bridge with crude hired equipment, Sexton had his troubles loading it but I had no trouble planting it. It took 7 hours to dig, load, and transport it 2 miles and about an hour and a half to plant it, plus 2 hours more to guy it off and paint the scars.[2]

By the next summer, Phillips was advising Sexton on the design, most specifically on the entrance to the garden and how a visitor should be introduced to the Hammock, as well as the "character of development within the Hammock."[3]

Phillips believed that the "first problem and perhaps the most important of all, is how to stop people who are driving down the open highway at sixty miles an hour. We have to catch their attention, to intrigue their interest, and finally to reward their interest." Phillips proposed a "striking change in the character of the roadside" that would include an expansive arrival along the highway and "distinctive, striking markers, or pylons of some sort, which can also be used as a brand or seal on all advertising matter, immediately associating the spot with the advertising."

Phillips said that he would "run a clipped hedge . . . along the Highway" and instructed Sexton to "let this hedge grow high enough to shut off from the view of passers-by in cars all but the tree tops of the Hammock, arousing interest as to what might be inside without revealing what is actually going on." To heighten the contrast, Phillips proposed a "neatly clipped" hedge with manicured grass as a backdrop to flowering shrubs. He also suggested that palms rise up behind the hedge. The contrast Phillips urged was not only between the Hammock within and the cultivated edge along the outside of the garden, but also between McKee and the rest of

Path winding through McKee Jungle Gardens.
Postcard, Rocco Ceo Collection.

the highway landscape. In that era, miles of hammocks still lined the highway, so the insertion of a refined hedge and floral display would have clearly signaled a new possibility.

Although he was unprepared to offer a specific

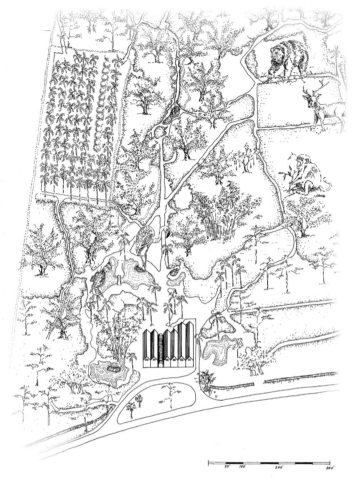

Detail of drawing showing entrance gate.

entrance gate design in the summer of 1931, Phillips demonstrated a conceptual understanding of the issues and the special qualities the gateway to a jungle might demand. He noted that the "Colonial Exposition is on in Paris," and as he would be visiting the Exposition, he believed he would find "some very jungly motives there." Phillips outlined his general concept of an entrance sequence that would

"give the visitor a brief resting spell," in preparation "for new sensations." After passing "through a corridor of some sort, walled densely enough on both sides, and roofed densely enough to shut them in for a few moments from what they have been seeing and what they are going to see . . . the jungle should appear in a striking, dramatic manner." He proposed two slat-sheds to form the corridor which would be a prelude to the jungle garden. "Then," Phillips told Sexton to:

clear the ground between the sheds and the Hammock of everything but the high trees, make a circular lawn about 100-120 feet in diameter, get this in brilliant green Rye grass for the winter and have exotic palms and whatever attractive plants you like around the edges (not, by all means, in the center).[4]

Phillips was adamant about the need for the open green at the center in order to establish the power of contrast. More poetically, he explained that:

as the visitor comes out from the corridor he will see the face of the jungle, brilliantly lighted in the afternoon or gloomily dark in the morning, across a bright pool of pure green, instead of behind a field of rough grass or tangled shrubs and vines as he has seen it along the highway. The effect wants to be a bit breathtaking. To get it you must have strong contrasts, and that involves a touch of artificiality. An artificiality not without

precedent in nature, for I have seen just such pools of brilliant green scum surrounded by high hammock and the effect was stunning.

Phillips also argued for a vista into the jungle, that "would go from a point on the far side of the lawn, opposite the corridor and in line with it straight on into the jungle for several hundred feet with a cut narrowing as it recedes, affording a deep mysterious view into the forest."

This sequence of spaces would produce "an introduction at once dramatic and inviting." Describing the process, Phillips imagined a visitor who would "enter the forest by degrees, crossing the fair lawn unapprehensive of snakes into a funnel still somewhat garden like as to the treatment of the ground along its sides, and find himself presently deep in the jungle and curious to see what lies beyond." Phillips believed that "nothing but rambling narrow trails through the Hammock" would "become monotonous." To avoid this he suggested:

a net-work of fairly direct paths giving a fair depth of vision ahead, particularly where the skyline along the trail is interesting. The paths should go from point to point of interest, as in the old French Royal Parks — not as avenues of course, but clearly direct. Some of them may be straight in the sense that you could pull a string-line through them somewhere even though the sides might be very irregular; others will ramble with sharp deflections like your present trails, may be those trails in fact. I would pick locations for them where interesting lines can be gotten without tree-cutting. I would not be afraid to cut shrubs if I could get a better effect thereby.[5]

In Phillips' construct for the garden, "the points of interest will be different sorts of growths, of which several can be found or can be made distinctive." He described a series of possibilities

"Never neglect the void; cherish it, defend it with troops, horse, and batteries. Nothing can be seen except through space. In aesthetics one must be bold and resolute..."

– William Lyman Phillips

including "oaks in openings surrounded by palms," which he believed could "be made into grassy focal points." Phillips listed for Sexton a planting strategy that would dramatize the native landscape so that one would see:

groves of oaks. . . single great oak trees; groves of palms where nothing but palms can be seen as far as the eye can penetrate; there are groves of palms surrounded close in by walls of low green trees and shrubs; there are palmetto swales which can be made into pods or grassy glades. The principle of contrast should not be overlooked. Do not be afraid to get out from

under the trees at times. The gloom of the forest will seem deeper if there are passages of sunlight.

Recognizing that "fear of snakes, which I have observed to fill the mind of the average winter visitor almost to overflowing, may be a real stumbling block," Phillips suggested "that the paths ought to have decent width, say 10 or 12 feet of clear ground" and should be kept clear so that the ophidiphobic might feel more secure if "they were walking clear of any brush or weedy growths." Phillips was careful to explain that he did not "mean that the trees would have to be cleared to a width of 12 feet, but only the low and shrubby vegetation," nor did he believe "that the clearing ought to be even; it would widen and narrow as circumstances might suggest."

The correspondence makes evident that Phillips was the principal strategist for the garden. He told Sexton that he didn't need "to discuss the planting you may want to do: Reinsmith can handle that all right. I do hope however that you will follow my general recommendation about the Introduction and the development of the Hammock, for I am sure it would produce a

most unusual and stunning thing."[6] The reply from Reinsmith indicates that Phillips' proposals were carried out to "a triumphant conclusion."[7] Calling Phillips' entry corridor "a knockout," Reinsmith reported that they were "doing great things along the highway front, changing the landscape much but adhering religiously to your counsels." After an ambitious summer of work, Phillips wrote to Sexton in October of 1931 to express his "admiration for the way you and your assistants have advanced the work in so short a time to a point where your faith in the possibilities of the hammock as a place of special beauty attractive to a wide range of public interest is already clearly demonstrated."[8]

The introduction of wildlife posed another consideration for the Gardens. Reinsmith, on

Postcard, Rocco Ceo Collection.

Bamboo root 'giraffe' at McKee entrance.
Photograph by William Lyman Phillips. Historical Museum of Southern Florida.

October 19, 1932, reported to McKee and Sexton on the state of the wildlife. They had:

freed the wild herons in accordance with a state law forbidding their retention in captivity over the mating season. They left for the marshes to the East, of course but we are somewhat compensated by the marsh hens that inhabit our woods. Likewise the otters escaped, our pens would not hold them. . . We turned the lone-star pheasant loose. . . Pheasant and quail do not like the dense cover of our woods but to keep them at all we should some day build a satisfactory aviary somewhere in the shrubby country near the deer pen . . . Our parrots, Dottie and Dodie, adorn the conservatory behind the fruit juice stand. . . The peacocks still strut about and are handsomer than ever. The turkeys

hatched two broods of which nearly a dozen remain, now almost full-fledged adults. . . The monkeys, Charlie and Susie, are as fine and mischievous as ever. . . It has been necessary to shoot many black snakes that sun themselves on the lily pads and lie in wait for a nice corpulent frog.

At this point, Reinsmith said that the Gardens had in their "catalogue 692 introduced species and 159 natives or a total of 851 species of interesting and very much alive plants which is very commendable for so young an enterprise in southern plants."

Over the next several years, the Gardens acquired a number of architectural elements. Phillips wrote to Sexton in April of 1935 to remind him that a "jungle garden, if it has architectural adjuncts, should have them of a bold, rugged character, primitive rather than expressing the last refinement of civilization." Perhaps due to distance, he refrained from the specific architectural proposals he built in other landscapes where he was on site. For McKee, Phillips said that "I'd hate to have it put up to me to demonstrate just what I would recommend to attain a bold, rugged, and primitive character, but I am sure it would not be an Ionic or Corinthian column."[9]

The pressure to increase holdings of plants and buildings grew with the Gardens' success.

Fearing that his carefully considered greens might disappear in response to that pressure, Phillips outlined for Sexton the crucial importance of the principle of contrast in garden design, with particular focus on the relationship of open space to planted edges.

Whatever merit is possessed by the thing I am proposing comes from the voids quite as much as from the mass of palms. Bear that in mind Waldo, the mass needs the void to be effective. Never neglect the void; cherish it, defend it with troops, horse, and batteries. Nothing can be seen except through space. In aesthetics one must be bold and resolute; he must realize that it is impossible to have everything in the same place; he must be prepared to sacrifice something somewhere. And when I say aesthetics I am not referring necessarily to some delicate, recondite beauty, but to the power of a thing to draw the eye, to stir the interest, to move the emotions, which is the kind of power we need here.[10]

A remarkably effective group of people combined their resources and their talents to enhance a naturally beautiful landscape and produce the powerful place that was McKee Jungle Gardens. The garden survived in its entirety until 1976, when sixty-two acres were sold and developed. Another confluence of talent and determination was needed to save the last eighteen acres. The remaining section of the original garden, which included the highway entrance and two historic structures, was finally rescued in 1995 by the Indian River Land Trust. Over the next six years, the Trust restored as much of the original vision as is possible within the smaller scope of the garden. The new landscape, reincarnated as McKee Botanical Garden was designed by David Sacks of Wallace Roberts & Todd in Coral Gables, Florida, and is based on his study of original drawings by Phillips, period photographs and accounts, as well as the correspondence among Reinsmith, Sexton, and Phillips.

An article of 1940 that appeared in *House and Garden*, called Florida itself "a garden" advising "visitors who have not time to explore large areas" that they could "enjoy the various tropical and jungle gardens scattered through the state." The author, Dorothy C. Kelly, singled out McKee, where "eighty acres of primitive Florida wilderness form a background for innumerable varieties of imported trees, plants and flowers— some native to the state and others brought from the outside. Spanish moss and rare flowering vines hang from the trees. Orchids gleam high overhead. . . It's a fascinating spot – well worth a visit."[11] Although the acreage today is reduced, the intent of the original garden can still be read in its newest incarnation.

–JL

Notes:

1. W.H. Reinsmith to William Lyman Phillips, Vero Beach, August 12, 1931, Research Center, Historical Museum of Southern Florida, Miami, Florida.

2. WHR to WLP July 23, 1930, Vero Beach, Research Center, Historical Museum of Southern Florida, Miami, Florida.

3. William Lyman Phillips to Waldo E. 4. Sexton, Lake Wales, June 4, 1931, 1, Research Center, Historical Museum of Southern Florida, Miami, Florida.

5. WLP to WES, June 4, 1931, 2.

6. WLP to WES, June 4, 1931, 3.

7. WLP to WES, June 4, 1931, 4.

8. WHR to WLP, Vero Beach, August 23, 1931, Research Center, Historical Museum of Southern Florida, Miami, Florida.

9. WLP to WES, Lake Wales, Oct 13, 1931, Research Center, Historical Museum of Southern Florida, Miami, Florida.

10. WLP to WES Miami, April 18, 1935, Research Center, Historical Museum of Southern Florida, Miami, Florida.

11. WLP to WES, August 7, 1938, Research Center, Historical Museum of Southern Florida, Miami, Florida.

12. Dorothy C. Kelly, "Jungles and Junkets," *House and Garden* (December 1940): 41.

Giant Cypress Stump at McKee Jungle Gardens

Postcard, Rocco Ceo Collection.

RAVINE GARDENS
1933 PALATKA, FLORIDA 1997
UNIVERSITY OF MIAMI · SCHOOL OF ARCHITECTURE

Drawing by: Margot Ammidown, Dale Deiner, Joannie Juarbe, John Litten, Dimitra Papadia, Daphne Peggs, Alex Plasencia, Robert Price, Galia Sanchez-Rosell, Marcelo Villabona, Eladio Walker
34¾" x 87½", horizontal format, ink on mylar, 1997

To pass through the rustic gatehouse at the entrance to the Ravine Gardens, formerly called the Azalea Ravine Gardens, is to embark on an experience filled with unexpected contrasts. The gently sloping green just beyond is bordered by a pergola of stone and

Garden pavilion at top of ravine.
Florida State Archives

logs along which fly the forty-eight flags of the states of the Union at the time the garden was built in 1933. This Court of Flags is aligned with a stone obelisk, sixty–eight feet

tall, centered near its entrance, and sets up a strong axis to a rustic log pavilion at the opposite end. The pavilion marks the end of the flat part of the site and announces the garden's steep descent.

From the pavilion, a visitor of the nineteen thirties had to negotiate a series of terraces that stepped down in small stages to the ravine's edge. From here one could make the steep descent into the ravine itself or choose to cross to its opposite bank by way of a suspension bridge of steel cable and wood. Whichever choice they made, those who ventured here in the early days of the gardens had a breathtaking view of the ravine. Its walls fall as much as 120 feet to the bottom. Such great depth is all the more impressive because it is unexpectedly encountered in a countryside characterized by only modest changes in elevation. The ravine walls are emblazoned with azaleas, which bloom during the months of February and March, the tourist season. Because the

Postcard, Rocco Ceo Collection.

garden is so deep, it can be appreciated in elevation as well as in plan and the azalea-blanketed walls of the Ravine provide spectacular color.

The Ravine Gardens are the product of a partnership between the federal government and local initiative. T. B. Gillespie, a road contractor who lived in Palatka, conceived the idea of transforming a great natural gash in the earth into a display garden. It is one of only a handful of gardens laid out in terrain shaped by water erosion. The seepage

SOME OF THE 105,000 AZALEAS IN RAVINE GARDENS, PALATKA, FLA.

Postcard, Rocco Ceo Collection.

from natural springs at the bottom of the now deep ravine formed the site into which extensive plantings, along with bridges and terraces, were introduced.

Gillespie engaged a Jacksonville landscape architect, Richard Forrester, to design these.[1] Arranging the placement of thousands of azaleas, exotic palms, japonicas, and japanese magnolias as well as numerous subtropical plants, Forrester selected plants from a fragrant and colorful palette. Forrester's artistry was made possible by the heavy work of men supplied during the Depression by the Federal Emergency Relief Administration (FERA), and the Civil Works Adminis-

tration (CWA). They cleared a dense tangle of vegetation covering most of the eighty-two acres within the garden, and Forrester then trained the crew to do the actual planting. The obelisk at the entrance to the garden was erected to commemorate the spirit of cooperation among the federal government in Washington, which supplied the labor, the city government, and the towns-people. A number of the original rustic log buildings have over time been lost but the stone obelisk and the pergola remain.

One of the more interesting features is a loop road five miles long that permits touring the garden by automobile. The road winds along the walls of the ravine and is partially hidden from the pedestrians above by the steep angle of the ravine's walls. Another feature is the series of suspension bridges that, in addition to the first bridge encoun-tered near the pavilion, transforms an ordinary walk into an aerial adventure.

The bridges are also a fitting reminder of the origins of the name Palatka, chosen in 1821 from an Indian word "Pilaklikala" which means crossing over.[2] The six miles

of paths accessible from these bridges provide access to a terraced stone and lawn amphitheatre that seats 3000 people. The visual drama of the garden made it a favored setting for beauty pageants that took place from the 1950s through the 1970s, and for the Palatka Azalea Festival, which still occurs each spring.

On January 1, 1970 the Ravine Gardens became part of Florida's state park system

Suspension bridge over bottom of ravine.
Florida State Archives.

Postcard, Rocco Ceo Collection.

that should be replaced, and to instill a vision of possibility for one of Florida's lost treasures. Future partnerships are needed to bring this garden back to its original glory.

–RJC

Notes:

1. Brian E. Michaels, *The River Flows North: A History of Putnam County, Florida* (Dallas, Texas: Taylor Publishing, [1976] 1986), 399.

2. Susan Clark, *A Historic Tour Guide of Palatka and Putnam County, Florida* (Palatka: Glanzer Press, 1992), 2.

through a deed to the State of Florida's Trustees of the Internal Improvement Fund, and although the basic lines of the garden are maintained, a great many original plantings and rustic outbuildings have been lost. The site is in dire need of funding to restore the garden to its historic condition and importance. While there is still much to enjoy in the garden, reconstruction of some of the original buildings and replanting would greatly enhance the effect.

More funds and more staff are needed to accomplish this. The drawing made by architecture students of the University of Miami attempts to depict what was lost, to serve as a graphic guide to the elements

Current view of walk along ravine.
Photograph by R. Ceo.

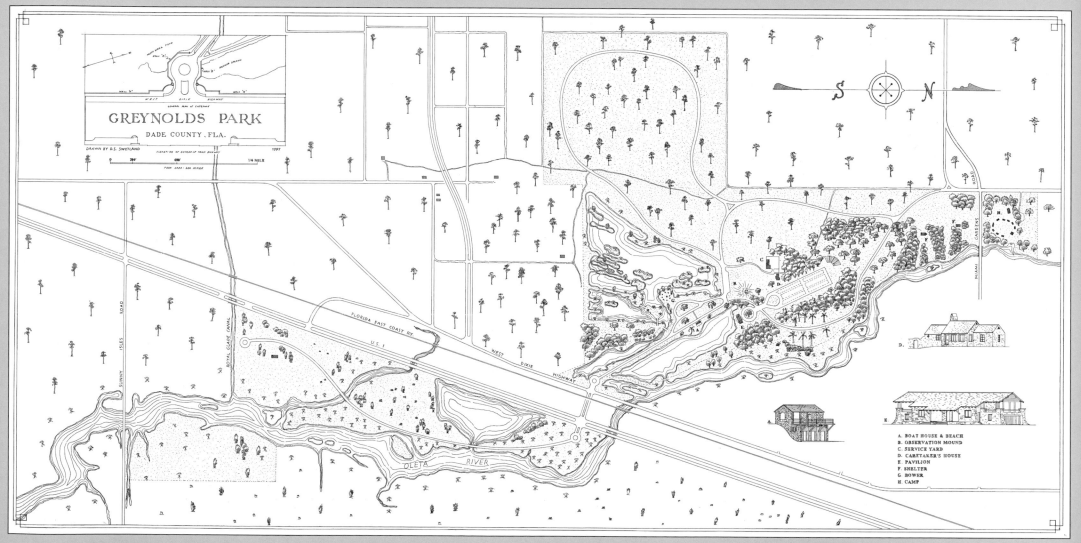

GREYNOLDS PARK

DADE COUNTY, FLA.

A. BOAT HOUSE & BEACH
B. OBSERVATION MOUND
C. SERVICE YARD
D. CARETAKER'S HOUSE
E. PAVILION
F. SHELTER
G. BOWER
H. CAMP

DRAWING BY: DAVID SWETLAND

24" X 48", HORIZONTAL FORMAT, PENCIL ON VELLUM, 1997

When William Lyman Phillips completed his work at Mountain Lake Sanctuary, he became a project superintendent for the Civilian Conservation Corps Camps (CCC) in what is now Miami-Dade County. Phillips worked first at Paradise Key, south of Miami, on the design and construction of Royal Palm State Park, at the southern edge of the Everglades.[1] After two years of work on Royal Palm, Phillips began work as the project superintendent for the U.S. Department of the Interior's National Park Service in its construction of Greynolds Park.

Initiated by Congress in 1933, the CCC worked concurrently with the Works Progress Administration (WPA). Familiar with the untrained workers from the Civilian Conservation Corps, Phillips reprised his role as designer, construction manager, and as a teacher in the art of drafting, surveying, and other necessary construction skills. Although the laborers of the CCC were not necessarily skilled in the task at hand, they were in Phillips words, "serious and industrious."

Oolitic limestone bridge, c. 1936.
Photograph by Gleason W. Romer. Romer Collection, Miami-Dade Public Library.

Phillips described the educational activities of the Camp which included "English, French, surveying," and he noted that the "Educational Adviser feels much pleased with the progress made in the reduction of illiteracy, especially since the advent of a very capable English teacher who has been loaned by the WPA." One aspect of the development of the members of the Corps however, was that as they advanced, they moved on, which Philips recognized was the purpose of the Corps, but nonetheless regretted that "the Camp is constantly losing its most useful workers."[2]

With his crew in training, Phillips opened an axis to lead visitors to the central feature of the park, which he described as a "striking observation mound."[3] After providing visitors with a promontory from which to take their bearings, Phillips then creates opportunities for other experiences through individual buildings in the woodland and access to various bodies of water. The interweaving of land and water, which Phillips presents clearly from the introductory observation point, is a concept that characterizes the overall plan of the park.

In one of his bi-monthly reports to the Department of the Interior about his work on the parks in Miami, Phillips explained that it was "important to note that in their natural state woods and field here are impracticable for play,

"The high vantage point not only permits the people to see more but it reveals in the scene interest and charms unsuspected from the normal points of view."

– William Lyman Phillips

picnicking, camping; often impossible to walk over with any pleasure."[4] Although Phillips found the site for Greynolds Park to be "unusually picturesque," he wanted to be sure that his Washington directors understood that the park suffered from:

the normal impracticable sort of surface, or worse, for much of it represented the chaotic aftermath of quarrying operations. With the objective of providing pleasant places to picnic, camp, or to stroll about – a park for day or afternoon outings – a vast amount of work was done by the Camp in clearing, smoothing and in bringing order out of disorder.[5]

Reminding officials at the Park Service that conservation figured largely in this project, Phillips explained that "by providing places and trails where people could assemble and walk about in comfort, assurance was secured that

Observation Mound and Tower, c. 1936.
Photograph by Gleason W. Romer. Romer Collection, Miami-Dade Public Library.

natural surfaces would be less likely to be entered upon and abused. Firebreaks and fire hazard reduction gave further protection to the native growths."[6] In addition to the preservation of native materials whose participation in the landscape was now structured, Philips looked to the site for architectural cues and materials and noted that a number of "caretaking facilities were built— a shed, house, water supply, latrines, boathouse and refreshment booth. All buildings were made of the native limerock from the property."[7]

Phillips reported on the growing public interest in Greynolds Park when he wrote to Washington in November of 1934. The "quarry crew" had succeeded "in removing the rock ridge which concealed the park entrance from the Federal Highway," and a number of Sunday visitors were exploring the grounds. Sounding somewhat surprised, Phillips recounts that among them were architects curious about the "handwrought use of native materials," which Phillips thought might inspire a new local style

of architecture. In the summer of 1935, he reported that Greynolds had been discovered by the Scouts, "who despite the summer mosquitoes, spend a day or several days and seem to find the environment properly alterative." He noted that in the photographs of the Scouts' use of the park that he was sending with his report "may be discerned portions of our stone-concrete table-bench combinations under heavy loading."[8]

By all accounts, the park's opening was a triumph. A.D. Barnes, Director of Parks, recorded that from the first week of the official park opening in 1936, it "became an overcrowded, overused facility."[9] The support facilities and amenities were subsequently expanded to meet the need.

The architectural qualities of the park come from Phillips' mastery of the project, especially his conception of the Mound as the most prominent feature. Phillips designed the Mound to form a curving tower of limestone from which one could view the park. As early as November of 1934 in one of his regular progress reports to the Park Service, Phillips described the potential impact of the Observation Mound and Tower. In a long and poetic passage, Phillips recounts the historical associations of the Mound:

which rules the scene with a graceful domination, the focal point of many vistas. . . the mass has an ever-changing, ever fascinating aspect as one moves around it, so that no matter where one goes in the Park his eyes are drawn to look again at the Mound; just as no

doubt the people's gaze is turned to Fujiama or Vesuvius, or Popocatypetl from every corner of the countryside. In the ascent the fascination persists. You feel you are climbing up to a very strong high tower. The walls of the rotunda rise sheer and boldly above you; at the foot of the stone ramp on the shady north corner the wind is shrewd like the Mistral whining round the ancient whitened keeps on the hills beyond Avignon. The ramps and steps have a solid, eternal look and feel.

Then Phillips turns more fully to the local condition and imagines the visitor:

who leans on the parapet and looks over the Park, over the far stretches of pineland to the north and west over the wide mangrove swamps glistening with streams and lagoons to the thin line of blue where tramp ships pass, he is [beguiled] to trace out the elaborate interpenetration of land and water. All impatience, all restlessness is gone, and one would be content to stay there hour after hour, so rich in new interest does the landscape become when viewed from this height—this height which would be insignificant in a hilly

Lagoon frontage, c. 1936.
Photograph by Gleason W. Romer. Romer Collection, Miami-Dade Public Library.

Blueprint from William Lyman Phillips' drawing of North Elevation of Boathouse, 1935.
Miami-Dade Park and Recreation Department.

Boathouse as seen from across the lake.
Photograph by R. Ceo.

region but which is a real eminence on the dead level of this coastal land.

Phillips proposes the height with its possibilities of distant views as a means of engaging the visitor in the natural landscape while still protecting a fragile site from human use. The balance between the native Florida rockland and public recreation would be a concern throughout Phillips' career and remains an issue in the present day. For Phillips however, at that moment, it seemed:

> *clear now, that regarded as a means of making natural scenery accessible to view with the slightest possible violation of Nature, the thing is unquestionably justifiable and right. The high vantage point not only permits the people to see more but it reveals in the scene interest and charms unsuspected from the normal points of view.*[10]

Frederick Law Olmsted, Jr. wrote to Phillips in January of 1935 to congratulate him on the success of the Outlook Mound and Tower. Olmsted commented that the "silhouette of the main body of masonry reminds me strikingly of the Chateau of Murols in Puy-de Dome or thereabout, though of course on a very much smaller scale. . . the thing itself seems to be a fine piece of constructive design; suitably theatrical

and arresting but very refined in line and composition."[11] The complexity of Phillips' historical associations, rendered at a more modest scale as Olmsted noted and in local materials as Phillips determined, would establish a method of design for Phillips' later work. Greynolds was the first of several major parks that Phillips would design for Miami-Dade County. The hallmarks of a Phillips project—relationships to important historic precedents, the integration of architecture and landscape, the use of local materials in the building and the landscape, punctuated with exotic introductions as details – are evident in the work at Greynolds and signal the beginning of his distinguished public career in South Florida.

–JL

Oolitic limestone Boathouse.
Photograph by R. Ceo.

Notes:

1. Faith Reyher Jackson, *Pioneer of Tropical Landscape Architecture: William Lyman Phillips in Florida* (Gainesville: University of Florida Press, 1997), 123.

2. William Lyman Phillips to National Park Service, "Narrative Report, Months of January 1935 and February 1935," National Archives, College Park, Maryland, RG 79, Florida SP-2.

3. WLP to NPS "Special Narrative Report, March 31, 1936," National Archives, College Park, Maryland, RG 79, Florida SP-2, Box #15.

4. WLP to NPS, March 31, 1936.

5. WLP to NPS, March 31, 1936.

6. WLP to NPS, March 31, 1936.

7. WLP to NPS, March 31, 1936.

8. William Lyman Phillips to National Park Service, "Narrative Report, Months of June and July 1935," National Archives, College Park, Maryland, RG 79, Florida SP-2, Box #15.

9. A.D. Barnes, 1986, "History of Dade County Park System 1929-1969, The First Forty Years," File 5-23:174, William Lyman Phillips Papers, Research Center, Historical Museum of Southern Florida, Miami, Florida.

10. William Lyman Phillips to National Park Service, "Narrative Report, Month of November 1934," National Archives, College Park, Maryland, RG 79, Florida SP-2, Box #15.

11. Olmsted to Phillips, 16 January 1935, File 7-5, William Lyman Phillips Papers, Research Center, Historical Museum of Southern Florida, Miami, Florida.

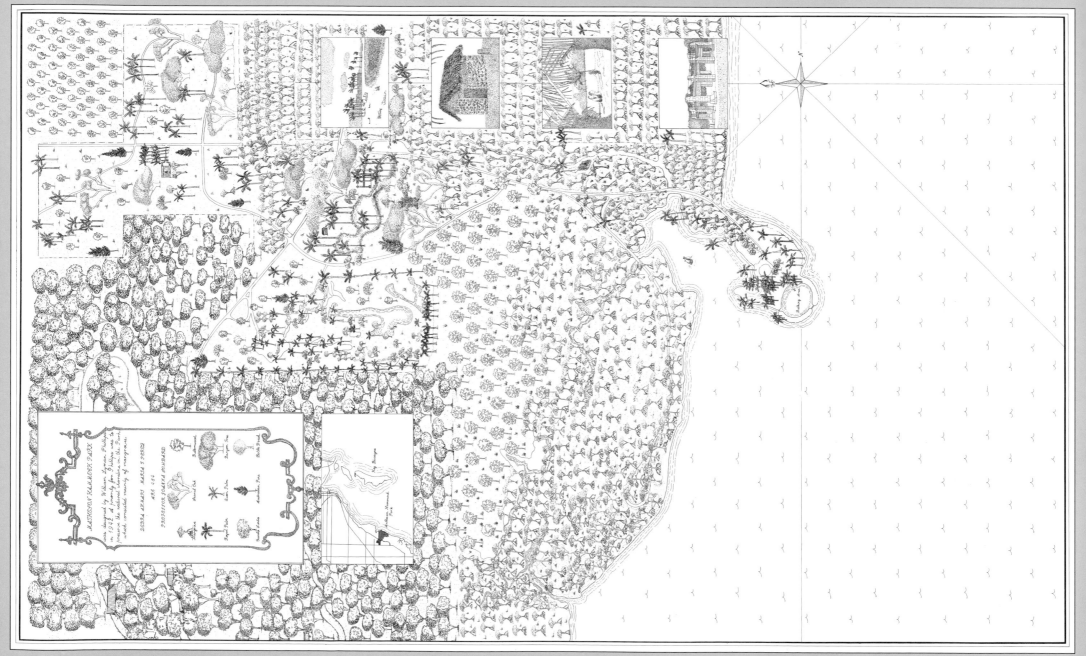

DRAWING BY: DEBRA AHMARI, MARITE PEREZ
30" X 48", VERTICAL FORMAT, INK ON MYLAR, 1998

In 1930 William J. Matheson and his son Hugh gave Dade County eighty-five acres of tropical hardwood hammock for a public park to be used as a botanical garden. The County then acquired an additional 420 acres of adjacent mangrove and hammock with a mile of frontage along Biscayne Bay.[1] The Civilian Conservation Corps (CCC) began work on the park in 1935 under the direction of William Lyman Phillips whose inventiveness in dealing with the numerous challenges of construction and the varied backgrounds of the CCC crew at Royal Palm State Park had prepared him fully to address the mangrove of Matheson Hammock.

In late spring of 1936, Phillips wrote a report to the National Park Service, which had been charged with supervision of CCC work in its own parks as well as in those of state and local governments. The objectives of Phillips' work at Matheson Hammock were to "protect the valuable natural forest reservation for which the Park was primarily established," and "to gain access across a wide swamp to the bayshore for the purpose of developing the exceptionally good water recreation possibilities."[2] Phillips

Trail through mangrove forest.
Photograph by R. Ceo.

intended that the "amount of natural surface modified for use and visitation will be relatively very slight. The park is primarily a nature preserve."[3]

One of the most challenging tasks at Matheson Hammock was the clearing of a road to the beach. In his October and November report in 1935, Phillips explained that the seemingly simple act of building an access road was really the enactment of the formal principle of contrast at work in the tropical landscape. To the unknowing eyes of:

the outsider, to those who later use the road, there is presumably nothing marvelous about it at all – there are so many miles of road in Florida built through marsh and swamp lands that the thing is commonplace. . .

But if it happens in a case like this that qualities of scenery somewhat commonplace have nevertheless aesthetic significance of a definite nature, though not obvious to everyone, it is worthwhile to call particular attention to them. The qualities here are the properties of a foil, of a contrasting element. . .The swamp is silent, windless, monotonous. Suddenly one comes out into the open of a quiet cove where low dark forest walls are reflected in still water, and the illimitable Bay is seen past a headland of high wind-moulded trees. It is as if one had passed through a dim chamber into a bright and splendid hall.

Continuing in the poetic language that one would not expect in a typical bimonthly progress report, Phillips directs his reader to the climactic moment that builds on the

Postcard, Rocco Ceo Collection.

Biscayne Bay waterfront, c. 1937.
Photograph by Gleason W. Romer. Romer Collection, Miami-Dade Public Library.

integration of underlying design principles and natural landscape. Now:

the swamp crossing has provided a few minutes of quieting detachment from humanized scenes, from any scene which would particularly attract the eye, so that the terminal incident comes with a freshness and vigor which would have been lacking if this special preparation had not been made. A different sort of contrast, and a stronger one, can be experienced where the road reaches the Bay shore. There the dead silence of the mangrove forest is suddenly broken by the "many-voiced tongue of the Sea," by the incessant lapping of wavelets on

the beach and that rattle of wind in foliage which is peculiar to tropical strands. The breeze is fresh and bracing, and the views seaward through the screen of fantastically contorted mangrove trees have a dramatic quality. It is a fine effect, one could almost say an exciting effect, and yet it must be dependent largely on the contrasting prelude, for if one came to this beach by the way of an ordinary bayshore boulevard he would scarcely experience any emotion when he arrived.[4]

Phillips was attentive to the vital role the mangrove played in the composition of the park and in the ecology of the Florida shoreline. He recognized that the loss of the mangrove would transform the coast forever obliterating any indications of its origins. Phillips thought it unfortunate, that:

the mangrove swamp is to most humans a hateful, hostile growth. Their first and only desire is to do away with it, preferably by a fill which replaces wet ground with dry and kills the trees. The growth is somehow incompatible with human habitation. It is a vanishing type of forest; the swamps year by year are pushed further away from the City. Yet, as a forest type, mangrove is unique; and where, in a given situation such as this, the swamp can be assigned an important role in a total park effect, and can be regarded and managed sympathetically,

the preservation and passing down of it to posterity would seem to be an act of considerable cultural significance.[5]

Phillips' road to the Bay unifies the park as it links the many and varied landscape experiences into a comprehensible whole. Once again, he draws upon principles of variety and contrast to heighten the differences among the park elements. Rustic shelters made of the native oolitic limestone are placed in grassy openings along the western lakes, while royal palms are used to mark the southern boundary of the park. The oolitic limestone concession stand next to the wading pool is more architecturally refined than the shelters. Each event is considered within an overall composition and is carefully orchestrated to produce a unified effect.

Oolitic limestone park shelter built by the CCC, c. 1937.
Photograph by Gleason W. Romer. Romer Collection, Miami-Dade Public Library.

Wading pool.
Photograph by R. Ceo.

The principles Phillips developed at Greynolds Park and Matheson Hammock, which draw upon the ordering concepts of unity, harmony, variety and contrast, would be refined further in the composition of the Hammock's near neighbor, Fairchild Tropical Garden. Although the uses of buildings have changed over the years and the number of visitors is far greater than what was projected in Phillips' era, the park still retains its original mission, to demonstrate the unique botanical conditions of a hammock landscape. The mystery and majesty of Phillips' passage through the mangrove is still "bracing." And in a manner much larger than Phillips predicted, not only the preservation of this mangrove, but the design of the park has become "an act of considerable cultural significance."

–JL

Notes:

1. Ellen J. Uguccioni, "Report of the City of Coral Gables Planning Department Historic Preservation Division to the Historic Preservation Board on the Designation of Matheson Hammock Park as an Historic District," March 1992, 2.

2. William Lyman Phillips to National Park Service, 31 March 1936, RG- 79, Box 15, National Archives, College Park, Maryland.

3. WLP to NPS, 31 March 1936.

4. William Lyman Phillips to National Park Service, Oct.-Nov. 1935, RG-79, Box 15, National Archives, College Park, Maryland.

5. WLP to NPS, Oct.-Nov. 1935.

CORAL CASTLE

1940

SUSAN BENNETT · LINDA FRANCO   · UNIVERSITY OF MIAMI ·   MYRENE GIULIANI · HAO K. MUBARKA
1995

STONEHENGE, ENGLAND

MOAI, RANO RARAKU, EASTER ISLAND

DRUIDS' TEMPLE CIRCLE, YORKSHIRE

DRAWING BY: SUSAN BENNETT, LINDA FRANCO, MYRENE GIULIANI, HAO K. SHAN
24" 36", HORIZONTAL FORMAT, INK ON MYLAR, 1995

It is a natural tendency for all living things to take it easy. You watch any living thing you want to, and you will see that as soon as they fill up, they will lie down and take it easy.[1]

These words from a book by Edward Leedskalnin, the builder and designer of Coral Castle, reflect his homespun philosophy and are indicative of his ideas for the design and construction of Coral Castle. This monumental construction from massive cuts of native coral rock is something of a wonder not only because he used remarkable techniques to assemble it but also because it is unique among Florida's landscapes. Tremendous will and unrequited love apparently supplied Leedskalinin with inexhaustible energy and ingenuity in pursuit of his dream, to build a shrine dedicated to the return of his lost love. Alone and shielded from view, he fashioned a highly idiosyncratic outdoor living space, part memorial, part astronomical observatory and part obsession.

Ed Leedskalnin at Coral Castle, then named "Rock Gate".
Courtesy of Irene Barr, Coral Castle.

Leedskalinin made it all with simple tools, using more than 1,000 tons of coral rock. The grounds contain a Polaris telescope twenty-five feet tall and weighing twenty-eight tons and a tower that served as his residence (243 tons). He embellished his Coral Castle with domestic objects of astonishing weights: rocking chairs one half ton each, a heart shaped table two and one-half tons with an ixora bush planted in its center so he would always have fresh flowers, a monolithic couch eight feet in diameter mounted on a Ford brake drum so it could be turned to follow the changing position of the sun.

His creation is a mixture of Stonehenge and folk art within a garden of plantings most often found in a tropical landscape. There is in Leekskalnin's rock garden some of the same monumental transformation of place found in the cutting of great canals for the watery gardens of Vizcaya and for Merrick's dream of Coral Gables as a tropical Venice. Leedskalnin's quarrying of rock on the site shares with many Florida landscapes a relationship to the ground that seems typical of the region: to make land or a place you have to manufacture it. To construct a monument to one's love: look no farther than what is before you; exert an iron will. The builder of Coral Castle concluded his book with the observation that:

People are individuals. For instance, if you want an excitement you will have to test the thrill yourself, or if you have a pain you will have to bear it yourself, or if you want to eat you will have to eat for yourself. Nobody can eat for you and so it is that if you want the things to eat you will have to produce them yourself and if

Photograph by Rocco Ceo.

you are too weak, too lazy, lack machinery and good management to produce them, you should perish and that is all there is to it.[2]

Leedskalnin's love never did return. The castle, weathering regular hurricanes, refuses to perish and sits stoically along US1 in Homestead waiting to tell its story to the visitor who happens through its gates.

—RJC

Rare view of Coral Castle under construction.
Postcard, Rocco Ceo Collection.

Notes:

1. Edward Leedskalnin, *A Book In Every Home* (Homestead, Leedskalnin, 1936), 22.

2. Leedskalnin, 1936, 26.

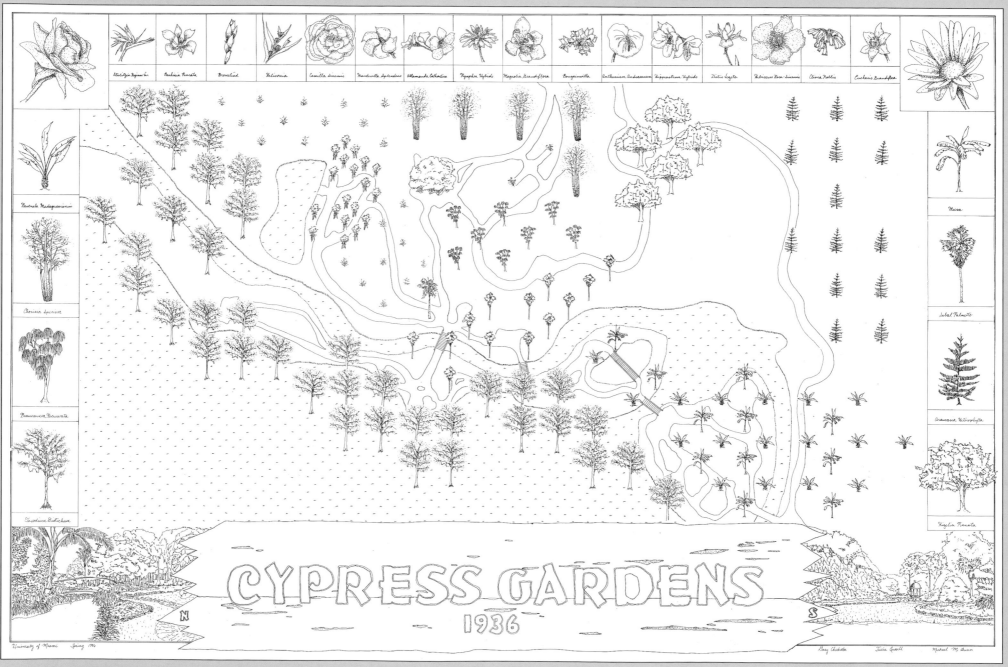

DRAWING BY: GARY CHICHESTER, MICHAEL MCGUINN, TRICIA RUSSELL
24" X 36", HORIZONTAL FORMAT, INK ON MYLAR, 1996

P erhaps the best-known attraction garden in Florida is Cypress Gardens in Winter Haven. Opened on January 1, 1936, the gardens are the product of the creative marketing ideas of Dick and Julie Pope who took a hillside site of thirty-seven acres on Lake Eloise and turned it into a major theme park that is now internationally famous.

Following an industrious start as the marketing director and salesman for Johnson Outboard Motors and two other prosperous positions in public relations in Chicago and New York, Dick Pope came to Florida after the stock market crash of 1929. Hearing about the success of a banker and plantation owner in South Carolina who had established a garden as a tourist attraction, he and his wife Julie, with their new baby, headed south to try their luck at improving on that idea. Pope's genius for marketing and love of water sports made their dream come true, but first he had to lay the financial foundations for it. He already had a vision of the garden and he had his eye on the site, which he purchased in 1931, but he lacked the funds to develop the project. On the basis of his past experience with boating and skiing, Pope landed a position on the Winter Haven Canal Commission. He soon approached its members with the idea of using

Photograph by R. Ceo.

operating funds from the Federal Emergency Relief Association (FERA), to build a public garden. After winning the support of the Chamber of Commerce and other civic clubs, he drummed up enough money to start his garden. Additionally, John Snively Sr. owned a yacht clubhouse on adjacent land and offered the building for use as part of Pope's scheme. But transforming the swampy site into a garden was no easy task, and the difficulties soon encountered when they tried to establish new plantings proved too much for the Commission. It pulled out after hearing that Edward Bok had spent three million dollars making his garden in Lake Wales. Locally, people scoffed at Pope's ambition.

With the flip of a coin and resolve to not look back, Richard and Julie Pope then formed the Cypress Gardens Corporation and continued to build upon their original idea. They worked hard themselves and were supported by friends, including George Jenkins, founder of the Publix grocery stores. Jenkins at one point gave Pope chits worth a dollar and a quarter apiece so that his workers could buy groceries. With such help from friends and a little creative financing, slowly the swamps were drained and hundreds of dollars worth of camellias and azaleas were planted.

Although the wonderful ancient cypress trees and picturesque gardens are still a good reason to visit the garden, there are now a variety of attractions

Postcard, Rocco Ceo Collection.

including "Southern Crossroads" which recreates a town of the Antebellum south, an animal nursery, an aviary, and an animal forest, as well as shows – bird, reptile, and magic shows – along with air dancing. There is also an island in the sky: to reach it and view the gardens from a sixteen-story height, a visitor is hoisted by a hydraulic arm attached to a counterweight made of 350 tons of concrete.

But the big draws of this tourist attraction remain the gardens themselves, the water-ski show, and the "Southern Belles." Girls beautifully costumed in billowing dresses of antebellum style first appeared in Cypress Gardens after a bad freeze burned many plants and Julie Pope came up with the idea of strategically placing these eye-catchers to distract attention from ruined shrubs and flowers. Her clever response to a minor emergency worked, and the girls remain, in lasting homage to the Popes' ingenuity in creating and defining the term "attraction garden."

–RJC

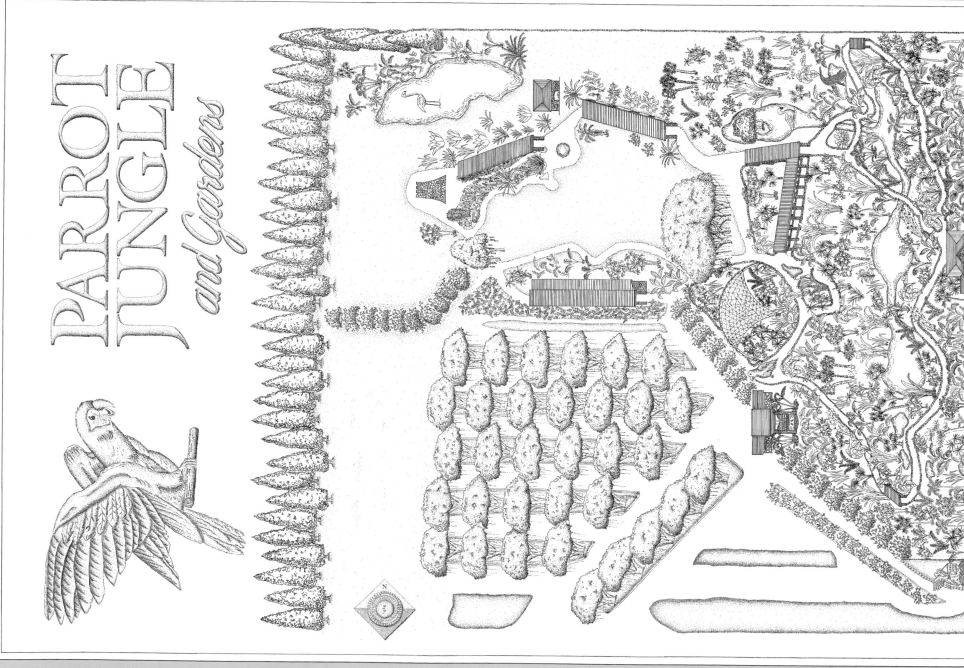

PARROT JUNGLE *and Gardens*

DRAWING BY: PAMELA MACE, JULIANNE NAPIER, MARIE V. TRIVIGNO

20" X 30", VERTICAL FORMAT, INK ON MYLAR, 1995

Banyan tree viewed from cactus garden.
Photograph by R. Ceo.

Scherr was instructed to drive up to South Miami and turn right at the town's only traffic light. He should then follow Red Road south along the Snapper Creek canal for a couple of miles. He found the property and pulled off the shoulder of the road, scattering a gang of bulbous blue and gray land crabs under the tires of his car. He must have immediately sensed that this was, even among the broad swathes of subtropical wilderness still existing in South Florida, an uncommon piece of land. From the roadside, towering cypress trees could be seen soaring eighty feet above the tangled underbrush and darker hammock. Craning

his neck he spotted what he guessed was an eagle's nest high in the bald cypress. A good omen.[1]

In 1936 Franz Scherr, the founder of Parrot Jungle, conceived a lofty dream and embarked upon the creation of a jungle garden of exceptional beauty. Like many men before him, Scherr had limited resources but an abundance of imagination. He felt that he just needed to find the right site. For his project, hammock landscapes with their natural jungle-like conditions were logical choices, but they were typically more expensive than pineland because they were already beginning to disappear in the 1930s. Hammocks provided deep shade, hardwood trees, and natural solution holes, ideal settings for dark jungle landscapes that contrasted nicely with the brilliant colors of the exotic birds.

It would have required years to create such landscapes on the rocky soil of pineland after the backbreaking job of clearing it. Orchid Jungle, Monkey Jungle, and Parrot Jungle were all cultivated within naturally occurring hammocks whose natural beauty and potential allure for

tourists were recognized by early pioneers who capitalized upon them. With imagination they transformed these found jungles into accessible landscapes that people would pay to see.

In 1936, Franz Scherr had already been a resident of Homestead for ten years, when he found the natural beauty of a cypress stand on twenty acres along Red Road, just a few miles from US1, and recognized an ideal site for parrots. The garden he constructed was originally entered from Red Road, which bounded it on the east, and was laced with trails that provided wonderful views of tropical plants and birds alike. Originally, guides led visitors, describing the gardens and birds, but over time the foot traffic increased so much that tours

Original Red Road entrance to Parrot Jungle.
Postcard, Rocco Ceo Collection.

another and compressed experiences. The originators employed classic garden devices including a graded, winding path to an overlook, a picturesque stroll with carefully controlled vistas, and a featured specimen such as a banyan tree, sausage tree, or albino alligator. All were woven together in a seemingly natural setting. Although Parrot Jungle's site is relatively small, the techniques that compress experience created the illusion of strolling the grounds of a much larger garden. The sensation of walking into another world was heightened by the contrast of the visitor's passage from the once ubiquitous, but now lost, pineland that had surrounded the garden, into the rich and dense hammock that simulated a tropical jungle.

Drawing detail showing geodesic dome.

began to bump into one another. The garden's popularity would eventually necessitate self-guided tours that accommodated throngs of tourists.

Bird shows were among the attractions drawing them there, staged under the geodesic dome of Parrot Jungle's theater, where birds rode roller skates, bicycles, and various other wheeled devices. This show, still being performed in 2001, was upstaged only by another show that is no longer presented, one that featured marching flamingos. These bizarre exhibitions of unnatural acts delighted the audiences, who came to be entertained.

The garden's layout allowed for a variety of simultaneous activities. A density of planting obscured the closely adjacent exhibits from one

Postcard, Rocco Ceo Collection.

Flamingo lagoon.
Photograph by R. Ceo

Watson Island is not a hammock. Without this time-honored traditional setting for the attraction, its new owners must begin with the re-creation of the jungle itself. It remains to be seen whether the new setting will recall the historic qualities so important to the original garden.

–RJC

Notes:

1. *Cory Gittner, Miami's Parrot Jungle and Gardens: The Colorful History of an Uncommon Attraction* (Gainesville: University Press of Florida, 2000), 7.

Postcard, Rocco Ceo Collection.

One of Franz Scherr's greatest triumphs was to train birds that were free to fly away. Through trial and error, and after many expeditions across Miami to retrieve escaped birds, Scherr succeeded in training the parrots to return by using a combination of regular feedings, properly chosen mates, and patience. One amazing aspect of Parrot Jungle is the constant reminder of its presence throughout the city. Once visitors have been to the Jungle, they need only see a pair of macaws flying along US1 to recall the garden. This is a landscape that has taken flight literally and metaphorically. Its future location on

DRAWING BY: SHANNON CROWELL, LANA PATRICIOS, COLETTE SATCHELL
27½" X 54", HORIZONTAL FORMAT, INK ON MYLAR, 1992

Emerging from the Civic Association of Palm Beach in January of 1936, the Society of the Four Arts was dedicated to fostering art, music, literature, and drama. Two years later, the society opened its first building, designed by Maurice Fatio, with an exhibition that included Rembrandt's painting, *Aristotle Contemplating the Bust of Homer*, and with the Palm Beach Garden Club's demonstration gardens in place.[1] Lee Rogers, in the *Palm Beach Daily News* on Saturday, February 26, 1938, described the opening that Friday afternoon, when "visitors stepped into a veritable realm of beauty in all imaginable forms of exquisite blooms, charming gardens and unusual trees and shrubbery." Rogers described the Chinese garden of Mrs. Lorenzo E. Woodhouse, and Dr. Edmund LeRoy Dow's Tropical Garden. "Most instructive and at the same time lovely to view," Rogers asserted, "is the Spanish Patio 'Fuenta Cristal' of Mrs. John Phipps."

Rose garden.
Photograph by R. Ceo.

Rogers observed that "Mrs. Clifford V. Brokaw's British Colonial received many words of admiration from visitors, while Mrs. Alfred Kay's garden of tropical and subtropical fruit trees illustrated their use as ornamentation." Rogers explained that "all these gardens are permanent and together form an exhibit of rare beauty."[2] Equally enthusiastic, the *Palm Beach Post* on that same morning, quoted Mrs. Horace H. Work, who presented a pergola garden, saying that she had designed it as a "fragrant moonlight garden." Working only with white blossoms, she had used a number of aromatic flowering plants including lilies and jasmine.[3]

The next year, the *Palm Beach Post* announced on Friday, February 17, 1939, that "two new gardens will augment the six permanent ones created last year for the flower show." One of the new gardens would be the work of Mr. and Mrs. Hugh Dillman, "and the other will be by the Garden Club to demonstrate border plantings, especially." The *Post* also reported that "the six original gardens are much more beautiful after a year's growth and development," and explained that "the purpose of these gardens is to demonstrate what plants will grow here and what type of plantings are suitable for the various types of architecture."[4]

The Garden Club had been formed in 1928 and six months later its members had experienced their first major hurricane. Many of them owned expansive gardens in the north and their encounter with a new, almost tropical climate inspired them a decade later to create models for the following generation.[5] On the basis of the original, successful demonstration gardens, the Four Arts Society included the president of the Garden Club as an ex-officio member to the Society's Board of Directors. On November 20, 1938, *The Palm Beach Times* remarked on the new association of the two organizations, pointing out that "the Palm Beach Garden Club is closely affiliated with the Society of Four Arts, and Mrs. Alfred G. Kay heads the former, and her husband the latter."[6]

By 1948, the Four Arts Society had acquired the Embassy Club, originally built in 1929 and designed by Addison Mizner. Palm Beach and New York architect, John Volk had been engaged in 1947 to remodel the building. The Embassy Club, across the street from the Society's Fatio building, would provide "a large and small gallery and a large director's room, . . . a workroom, with a new small kitchen for refectory purposes," as well as "a suite of executive offices."[7] The Society also gained a new auditorium, the result of "throwing a roof over the old patio." Also mentioned is the work of Wyeth, King and Johnson, the architects designated to "make the former Four Arts building into a library."[8]

As the architectural work progressed, the *Palm Beach Post* on March 25, 1948, reported that Ruth Sage, landscape architect, was assisting with

Spanish facade.
Photograph by R. Ceo.

reconstruction, "with all signs of hurricane damage removed." South Florida had been hit by a hurricane in late September of 1947 and then another large storm in October.[9] The combination of the Garden's age and related issues of maintenance, with the destruction of the storms, presented the Garden Club members with a challenge. Mrs. Lorenzo Woodhouse, who had consistently maintained her garden, "replanted and reconditioned the Chinese Garden at her own expense," while the "south area" was "the focal point of the reconstruction project. A number of tropical trees and shrubs, together with considerable smaller planting, have been added near the south entrance to the

gardens." A "striking innovation was the removal of the road west of the jungle garden and the planting of this area in material in keeping with that of the Dow project."[10]

Once the original demonstration gardens had been restored, the Garden Club developed an ongoing program of maintenance and a plan for improvements. In the spring of 1956, the Garden Club engaged the New York landscape firm, Webel, Innocenti and Webel, to develop a master plan for the grounds that would enhance the original demonstration gardens as well as provide an overall, unified structure. Richard K. Webel, a graduate of Harvard College, Harvard's graduate program in landscape architecture, and a Fellow at the American Academy in Rome, had formed a landscape firm with Umberto Innocenti in 1931. Renowned for their work with formal gardens long after other landscape architects had abandoned such a practice, Webel and Innocenti were prepared to detail the historic gardens appropriately and to propose new connections and additional garden elements sympathetic to the original intentions.

Webel described the project in the Garden Section of the Sunday *New York Times*, February 22, 1959, noting that "the gardens of the Four Arts in Palm Beach, Fla., although situated in the heart of the city, offer an oasis of beauty for all to enjoy." He had found an audience for the

gardens that ranged from artists and horticulturalists to the general public. Referring to the designs he first developed in 1956, Webel believed that the implementation of the new master plan "retains the individual gardens, but unifies the area and knits together the varying elements. This arrangement provides a more spacious open fountain area as a foil for the relatively smaller scale of the other garden units."[11]

Later in 1956, the Society had expanded its exhibition space across the street into a new garden with the acquisition of three additional lots just east of the former Embassy Club. The properties were slated to become a grocery store and then a parking lot before the Society rescued the land. Philip Hulitar, a member of the Society's Board who had been instrumental

Chinese Garden viewed from Moonlight Garden.
Photograph by R. Ceo.

Boxwood Garden.
Photograph by R. Ceo.

in the acquisition, had proposed using the land as a sculpture garden.[12] Newly arrived in Palm Beach from a successful career in New York as a fashion designer for Bergdorf-Goodman, Hulitar had the vision, ability, and commitment to design and install the Sculpture Garden.[13]

The significant role of the Four Arts Garden as an instructive force in local horticulture is evident in the many articles about the Garden that have appeared in local and regional media. The Garden expanded the Society of the Four Arts' quartet of art, music, literature, and drama, to include a fifth art, landscape gardening. Members of the Garden Club, in their association with the Society of the Four Arts, may have laid claim in Palm Beach to the lofty position that Thomas Whately, writing in the eighteenth century, declared was proper to gardening. "In the perfection to which it has been lately brought" he found that landscape gardening was:

entitled to a place of considerable rank among the liberal arts. It is superior to landscape painting, as a reality to a representation: it is an exertion of fancy; A subject for taste; and being released now from the restraints of regularity, and enlarged beyond the purposes of domestic convenience, the most beautiful, the most simple, the most noble scenes of nature are all within its province.[14]

–JL

Notes:

1. Olivia Gazzam Morrish, *A History of The Society of the Four Arts, Palm Beach, Florida: A Narrative of Significant Events from 1936 to 1983.*

2. Lee Rogers, "Palm Beach Flower Show is a Veritable Realm of Beauty," *Palm Beach Daily News*, Saturday, February 26, 1938.

3. "Crowds Put Seal of Approval upon 10th Flower Show: Exhibit This Year Is Smaller But Staged With Unusual Merit," *Palm Beach Post*, Saturday Morning, February 26, 1938.

4. "Two New Gardens Planned For Show," *Palm Beach Post*, Friday Morning, February 17, 1939.

5. Mrs. Alfred G. Kay, "History of the Four Arts Garden," *The Four Arts Garden: History and Catalogue of Important Specimens* (Palm Beach: The Garden Club of Palm Beach, 1978), 6.

6. "Four Arts Society has Gained Prominent Pace in Resort Program; Opens Dec. 1," *The Palm Beach Times*, November 20, 1938.

7. "Work On the Four Arts Building Begun," *Palm Beach Sun*, Friday July 25, 1947.

8. *Palm Beach Sun*, Friday July 25, 1947.

9. http://weather.unisys.com/hurricane/atlantic/1947/index.html

10. "Garden Club Views Reconstruction Work in Four Arts Society Gardens," *Palm Beach Post*, Thursday, March 25, 1948.

11. Richard K. Webel, "Gardens to Visit: Tropical Plantings in Palm Beach Inspire Artists and Hobbyists," *The New York Times*, February 22, 1959.

12. Olivia Gazzam Morrish, *A History of The Society of the Four Arts, Palm Beach, Florida: A Narrative of Significant Events from 1936 to 1983.*

13. Mrs. Philip Hulitar, telephone interview, 12 June 2001.

14. Thomas Whately, *Observations on Modern Gardening, Illustrated by Descriptions*, 3rd Ed. (London: T. Payne, 1771), B.

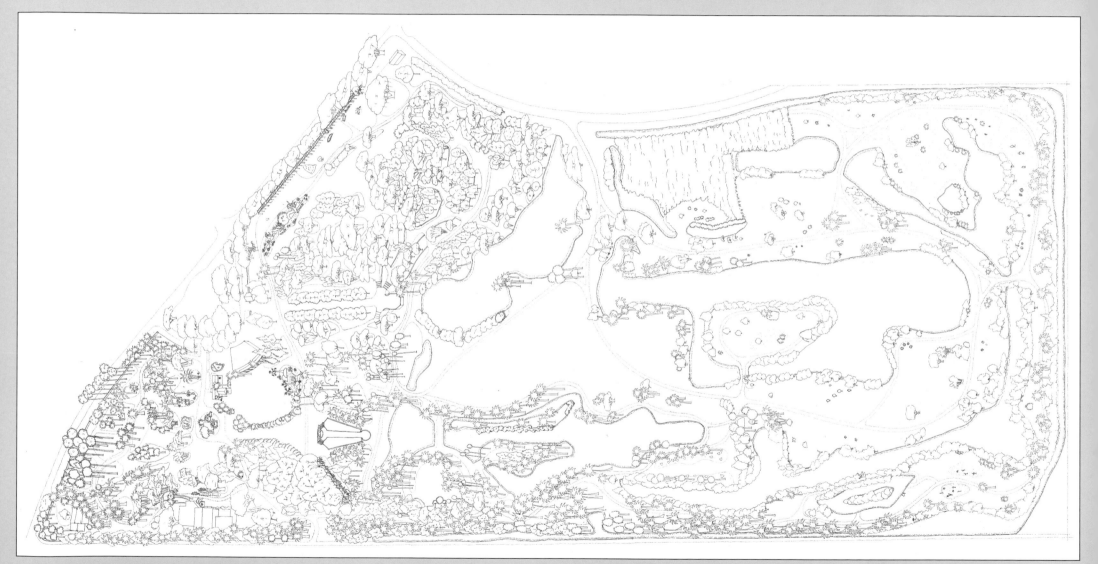

DRAWING BY: MOHAMED ABD RAZAK, GERALDINE CHONG, JASON NICHOLAS
36½" 49½", VERTICAL FORMAT, INK ON MYLAR, 1992

Colonel and Mrs. Robert H. Montgomery, with their gift of eighty-three acres, created Fairchild Tropical Garden. To enable county staff to assist in the development of the garden, the Montgomerys deeded fifty-eight of those acres adjoining Matheson Hammock Park to the County and deeded the remaining twenty-five acres, today referred to as the Montgomery Palmetum, along with 200 species of palms and flowering trees as well as funds to build improvements, to the new entity, Fairchild Tropical Garden.[1]

Colonel Montgomery in his remarks at the dedication on the 23rd of March 1938, identified the group of friends who first met in 1934 with the idea of starting a botanical garden in honor of David Fairchild, the renowned plant scientist, explorer, and collector. Charles Crandon, a Dade County Commissioner, pledged that the county would "cooperate 100% in this very meritorious enterprise."[2] Elmer D. Merrill of Harvard's Botanical Collections, who was acting supervisor of the Arnold Arboretum in Massachusetts, had also come to speak at the ceremonies. He reminded the audience of the

Montgomery Palmetum.
Photograph by R. Ceo.

importance of plants in civilization and predicted a bright future for the Garden.

Although the designer was not one of the speakers that day, William Lyman Phillips, with Noel Chamberlin, a landscape architect and friend of Colonel Montgomery, developed a preliminary plan for the garden which was published with the "Dedication." That plan depicts the skeletal structure of what would eventually take shape. The main overlook extended from what was then the entrance and established the central vista. A parallel axis of secondary importance began with what was planned as a director's house and extended a view out over a smaller lake. The two parallel vistas were linked by smaller paths and occasional views between them. A garden room at the east end of the overlook then had visual links to small clearings to the north and south.

At the outset of the project, Phillips wrote many reports which explained his strategy for the design of Fairchild Tropical Garden. He compared the shape of a botanical garden to the architecture of a museum and noted that "a museum consisting entirely of large salons" was less practical than one with "corridors and long galleries." He suggested that a botanical garden could afford, "as most museums can afford, a few

From Dedication of Fairchild Tropical Garden, March 23rd, 1938.
The William L. Phillips Papers, Archives and Special Collections, Otto G. Richter Library, University of Miami.

large rooms in which large and particularly fine pieces can be viewed from a distance. . . even if they are only 50 or 75 feet in diameter."[3]

Phillips believed foremost in "the principle of contrast, as expressed by the opposition of solids and voids and of relative degrees of solidity and vacancy—using contrast to attain variety."[4] In the Garden, the elaboration of the voids was achieved with open lawns, the turf floor of major garden rooms, the lakes, low profile plantings, and any concavity that would contrast with the vertical profiles of the major trees.

As an employee of the county, Phillips supervised workers of the Civilian Conservation Corps (CCC) in the building of the Garden wall, the

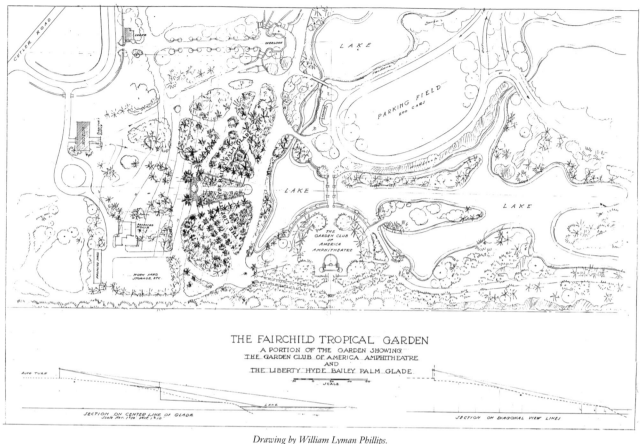

THE FAIRCHILD TROPICAL GARDEN
A PORTION OF THE GARDEN SHOWING
THE GARDEN CLUB OF AMERICA AMPHITHEATRE
AND
THE LIBERTY HYDE BAILEY PALM GLADE

Drawing by William Lyman Phillips.
Reproduction, Fairchild Tropical Garden Collection. Original, Miami-Dade Park and Recreation Department.

vine pergola, and Palm Glade which was dedicated to Liberty Hyde Bailey.[5] Bailey, a former assistant to the renowned botanist Asa Gray, had achieved his own national stature as founder and dean of Cornell's College of Agriculture and Life Sciences. The leading force in establishing botanical science as the foundation of academic horticulture, Bailey was the author and editor of hundreds of publications, among them, the Rural Science series which presented theories of landscape design to the general public. The close association

between science, horticulture, and design that distinguished the early part of the twentieth century was fundamental to Phillips' work.

With his significant range and his active role in the design, construction and installation of the Garden, Phillips' note to Colonel Montgomery in June of 1942 could have changed the future of the Garden. Explaining that the "Dade County Park Division has now been cut back to within an inch of the ground," Phillips wryly noted that he was "among the severed portions."[6]

Montgomery then retained Phillips to continue his work as the landscape architect of the Garden, a post Phillips held until 1954.

When Nixon Smiley assumed the directorship in 1956, he asked Phillips to record the principles of the Garden's design for future generations. Phillips set to work and produced what he called a "memoir" in September of 1958, subsequently published as an article in the journal *Landscape Architecture* in January of 1963. Phillips recalled that his first decision was to choose the principal "families" of plants to be exhibited. He determined the tropical basis of the collections, and made the decision to exhibit large shrubs and trees in families.

The property was "divided into a northerly half under one ownership (Dade County) and a southerly half under another." The uplands, "a strip about 500 feet wide on the northerly half and 800 feet wide on the southerly half," was at an elevation of about eighteen feet above sea level with "a strong slope or escarpment face 100-200 feet wide joining it to the lowland."[7] Phillips described the upland as "the edge of an ancient marine terrace which appears as an abrupt cliff at other points along the Biscayne Bay shore. The escarpment was the boldest topographical feature and strongly influenced the planning."[8] Phillips' determination to reveal the escarpment and to extend the major axes of the

Overlook and Palm Glade out over the lowland unified the landscape into important and memorable spaces.

To contrast with the geometry of the major axes, Phillips planned informality in garden plots, a strategy that "offered the utmost freedom in the choice of vegetation."[9] A subsequent formal element, the Garden Club of America Ampitheatre was planted to "demonstrate the use of particular species for compositional purposes."[10] The site's original plant material of pines and live oak did not assume great importance in Phillips' thinking, although the presence of "a number of old mango, avocado, and sapodilla trees on the Palmetum site did affect the layout to some extent. So did three sink holes, one in the Palmetum and two on the County side." Phillips noted that the escarpment's bare rock face had been a major inspiration, leading him to design a system of terraces with "stone walls retaining earth fills, forming plots elongated along the sidehill," which when planted would "form an effective windbreak " on the north side of the Overlook. Phillips also shifted the angle of the passages between the northern plots to deflect the north wind further.[11]

Phillips' plans for the lowland relied upon the flat open spaces needed to extend the axial views from the Overlook, and later from the Bailey Palm Glade, to the horizon. "The entire plan," he wrote "is essentially an articulated complex of openings."[12] Phillips felt that "the necessity of open spaces was obvious, for without well defined openings no sense of organization, no scenic effects, would be possible." Unlike the broad axial views of French formal gardens, the Fairchild vistas were narrow, but Phillips had discovered that "in Florida small landscape units and close views of vegetation are apt to be more attractive than wide views, and walks in the shade more agreeable than walks in the sun."[13]

Another of the formal principles governing Fairchild's design, "Variety," depended on the relationship of the major openings with the garden plots. "Consistency," which led to "unity" or "harmony" was achieved by the participation of individual parts in a designed whole. Most important to Phillips, the principle of "Contrast" established the relationship between the large vistas and the "close, intimate views on the upland," sunny openings and shady passages, as well as the contrast between the expansive panoramas—those of the Overlook, the Bailey Palm Glade, and the connecting views—with the narrow and shaded pathways that linked them.[14]

Following the tradition that Charles Eliot had established fifty years earlier, Phillips extended his supervisory role to include architecture.

In his report of 1958, Phillips discussed several architectural elements including the pergola that hosted a collection of vines given by a committee chaired by Mrs. John Semple, one of the Garden's early supporters. Clarence Dean, architect of David and Marian Fairchild's home, The Kampong, and landscape architect Noel Chamberlin consulted with Phillips about the design of the pergola.[15] Phillips felt that the

1941 view of Liberty Hyde Bailey Palm Glade

structure had not solved "the problem of displaying vines in all of their potentialities — some of them being capable of almost unlimited growth."[16] With architect Montgomery Atwater, Phillips produced the oolitic limestone gatehouse that served as the Garden's entrance and gift shop for a number of years. Later, when the Garden raised funds to build other structures, Phillips' role was less directly supervisory so that

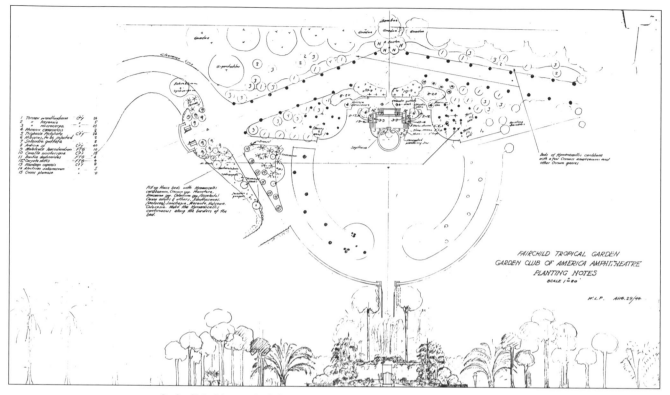

Garden Club of America Amphitheatre planting notes. 1944 Drawing by William Lyman Phillips.
Reproduction, Fairchild Tropical Garden Collection. Original, Miami-Dade Park and Recreation Department.

by 1939, the Garden engaged the architect Robert Fitch Smith to design a museum building and in 1946, an assembly hall known as the Garden House.[17]

Although Phillips regretted that the new construction eventually had shifted the Garden entrance to what he considered a service area, he was happier with the results of the Bailey Palm Glade in which "the narrow east end of the trapezoid would not let in much of the unwanted northeast wind, and the broad upper end would make possible a standing place where

people could take in the view down the lake." Phillips knew that the sunken garden below could not be filled with large palms, "without invalidating the viewing purpose," and advised caution. Phillips' concept of the Palm Glade required "cutting through the woods two diagonal avenues centered on the viewing position," so that "the whole plot would acquire a certain integration and might then be regarded as a palmglade." He recommended planting the sides of the trapezoid with palms and underplanting the oak woods "with shade-demanding species of palms." Phillips' later revision of the glade

extended the entire composition to the west with a curving avenue of cycads.[18]

While Montgomery had experimented with setting the palms in a lawn, Phillips believed that a forest floor was the ideal setting for the tree plots. He thought that grass should be restricted to specifically designed lawns in order to heighten the contrast between the dense plots and the open spaces.[19] Determined that the lowlands, upon which the Overlook and Bailey Palm Glade vistas rely, be preserved as open space, Phillips suggested a tropical forest-like development for some of the remaining lowland areas. His description of the tropical plantings is punctuated with strong compositional concepts, such as contrast and variety. He explained, for example, that one might find "light-toned trunks rising from a bushy cover, or seen against a solid green background." This was the effect he had "in mind . . . for the central lake . . . referring particularly to the island."[20]

Phillips felt that the upland relationships of alternating strips of lawns with the mulched, wooded plots would be impractical in the lowland where high water would wash the ground away. Instead, he proposed "herbaceous and shrubby ground covers," which would lead to "a wilder, more natural place than the upland." This strategy would allow "dense growth" that "would attain a stability similar to that of the

Palm glade.
Photograph by D. Hector.

dune hammocks . . . where maintenance in any ordinary sense is out of place."[21]

Phillips concluded his report on a note of concern for the future. "For the upland, it would seem desirable to search for plants of low or moderate growth suitable for underplantings, and for small shrubs and trees suitable for outside positions in the plots."[22] He urged as "the first concern of any administration" the maintenance of "the integrity of the open spaces." And he recognized the difficulty of dealing with change. Given the garden's location in the hurricane belt, he urged an awareness of the susceptibility of large mature trees to wind damage. He proposed that the Garden consider "a system of replacement, starting young trees to replace eventually the older ones,"[23] while recommending vigilance to suppress volunteer

plants so that the main lines of the overall garden structure would not be blurred and blunted.

With a close understanding of the site, Phillips applied landscape principles that engaged both the native context as well as the exotics that distinguish Fairchild Tropical Garden. Phillips' ability to magnify the qualities of a particular place, and simultaneously engage larger historical tradition, is his great gift to the landscape of South Florida. His masterful display of that ability at Fairchild Garden continues to engage visitors and to distinguish Fairchild Tropical Garden as an important cultural institution.

–JL

Notes.

1. Marjory Stoneman Douglas, *Dedication of the Fairchild Tropical Garden, 22 March 1938* (Miami: Fairchild Tropical Garden, 1938), 2.

2. Ibid., 3.

3. Phillips to Dahlberg, 27 July 1938, File 6-3, William Lyman Phillips Papers, Research Center, Historical Museum of Southern Florida, Miami, Florida.

4. Ibid., 2.

5. Phillips to Montgomery, 17 July 1941, File 13-11, William Lyman Phillips Papers, Research Center, Historical Museum of Southern Florida, Miami, Florida.

6. Phillips to Montgomery, 3 June 1942, File 13-11, William Lyman Phillips Papers, Research Center, Historical Museum of Southern Florida, Miami, Florida.

7. William Lyman Phillips, "The Fairchild Tropical Garden: A Memoir," 3 September 1958, File 13-1:4, William Lyman Phillips Papers, Research Center, Historical Museum of Southern Florida, Miami, Florida.

8. Ibid., 5.

9. Ibid.

10. Ibid., 6.

11. Ibid.

12. Ibid.,7.

13. Ibid.

14. Ibid., 8.

Entry gate by William Lyman Phillips and Gate House by William Lyman Phillips and Montgomery Atwater, 1939.
Photograph by J. Lombard.

15. Ibid., 18.

16. Ibid., 14.

17. Ibid., 10.

18. Ibid., 12.

19. Ibid., 17.

20. Ibid., 20.

21. Ibid., 21.

22. Ibid., 22.

23. Ibid., 23.

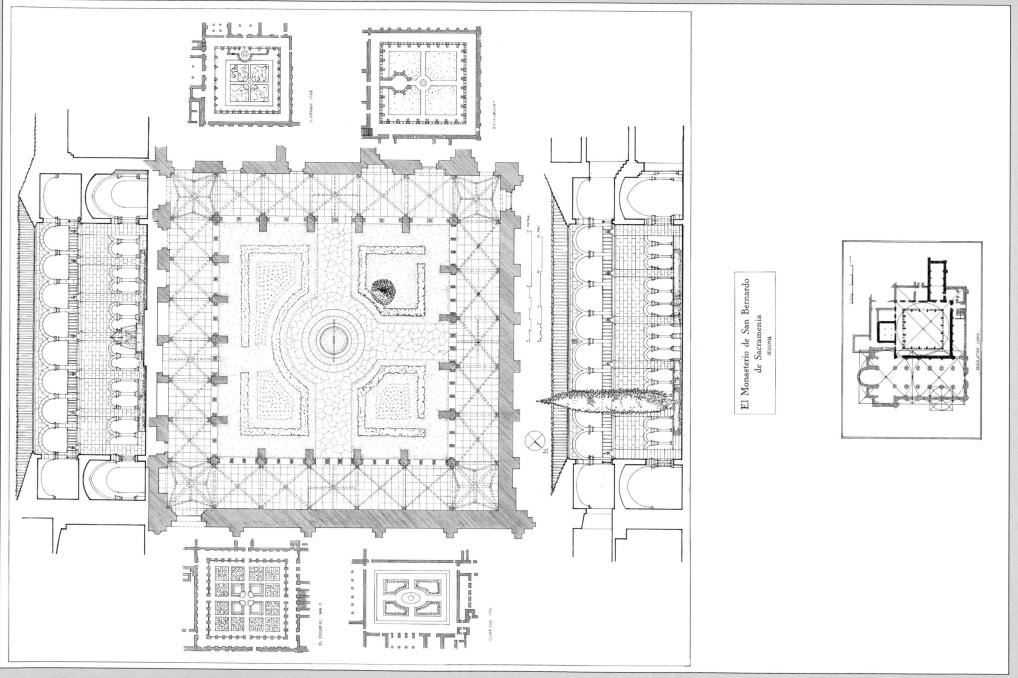

Drawing by: Paula De Carolis, Lino J. Iglesias
24″ x 36″, vertical format, ink on mylar, 1997

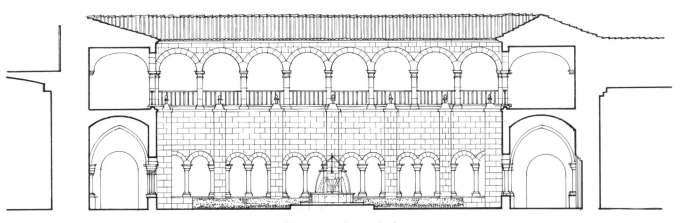

Cloister section, drawing detail.

Late in December of 1952, the *Miami Daily News* announced that "greater Miami's million dollar monastery jigsaw puzzle" had finally met its match. Reporter Larry Birger described "Allan Carswell, world-renowned stone mason" smiling "as he viewed the entire expanse of almost 33,000 pieces of the Cistercian monastery laboriously uncrated from 10,751 packing crates." Carswell, who had erected "The Cloisters" in New York for John D. Rockefeller, believed he would be able to lay the first stone, "within two to three weeks." One of the project's owners, E. Raymond Moss, hoped to have the site open to tourists in the next season.[1] According to an "Old Spanish Monastery" press release from the period, the reassembly actually took Carswell nineteen months and cost over one million dollars.[2]

Twenty-six years earlier, William Randolph Hearst had planned to rebuild the twelfth-century cloister from the monastery as part of a collection of buildings on the grounds of San Simeon, his grand estate in Northern California. Forced to abandon the scheme when he suffered financial setbacks, Hearst left the pieces in a New York warehouse. After Hearst's death, the crates of stones were sold to a group of investors who intended to reassemble the cloister as a tourist attraction. E. Raymond Moss, of Fort Lauderdale and Cincinnati, with William S. Edgeman, and later partners Carrol Muccia and E.K. Bludworth, were the principals in the purchase.

The cloister that inspired all this attention had come from a Cistercian monastery built in Sacramenia, in the Province of Segovia, Spain, in the middle of the twelfth century. After serving the Cistercian monks for almost 700 years, the grounds and buildings were confiscated and sold to a local wheat farmer. Arthur Byne, who acted as William Randolph Hearst's agent in the acquisition, wrote to him in October of 1926 about difficulties that had arisen locally. The project to move the monastery to America was being denounced to the Spanish Minister of Fine Arts. Byne's effort to keep the story out of the Spanish press was complicated by the unseating of his chief advocate, an artillery general, unfortunately positioned in a revolution by the artillery branch of the Spanish army. Byne reiterated a passionate request for the "ten thousand dollars of the twenty five asked for in May," and then for another twenty.[3]

Arrival in Florida of crates containing "Old Spanish Monastery" pieces.
Historical Museum of Southern Florida.

Cloister section, drawing detail.

Permission to remove the cloister and the refectory was only the first challenge. The building had been encased within a brick barn, and the stones had first to be retrieved from that enclosure, then disassembled in Spain, before being crated and shipped. The story of the unpacking of the crates in New York that mixed all the pieces just added to the puzzle. Then Hearst's own change of fortune which ultimately resulted in the stones' coming to Miami rather than to San Simeon added another layer of confusion. In all this, one important part of the puzzle remained elusive — the features of the cloister garden.

The architecture had been well documented, not only for this abbey, but also for many other illustrious Cistercian abbeys that held to a

rigorous order for seven centuries. Historian Wolfgang Braunfels identified St. Bernard's own abbey as the model. Abbots of other monasteries sent emissaries to Clairvaux with instructions to measure and document the buildings so that they could replicate them locally.[4] Braunfels credits much of the success of this paradigm to a design that "makes it possible to align delicate arcading in front of the bases of massive buildings of different dimensions — as the church and conventual buildings are — to produce the effect of a mighty load over something fragile,"[5] a feature visible in the reassembled cloister in North Miami.

The qualities of light, proportion, and acoustical resonance that distinguish Cistercian buildings are answered in their landscapes by water.

Medievalist Paul Meyvaert describes the choices of beautiful and secure sites for Cistercian monasteries, and "since agriculture was their main occupation they chose places where water and fertile land could be found."[6] According to Meyvaert, "the Song of Songs, so full of garden imagery, was a favorite source of spiritual

Cloister and garden shortly after completion.
Historical Museum of Southern Florida.

Central well representing the Tree of Life.
University of Miami School of Architecture.

inspiration for them."[7] The Tree of Life in the center of the Garden of Eden is represented in Cistercian cloisters through a central water feature such as a fountain or well. Christian theology alters the idea of life bearing water in Eden through the baptismal font which represents eternal life in Christ.

The cloister garden, by representing the new covenant of Christianity, reconsiders Eden as a potential that might yet await the faithful. Other traditional representations of Eden have quadripartite landscapes, with trees of sustenance and pleasure amidst a carpet of green that is enlivened by running water from a central font. Such images connect the monastic participant with the prospect of heavenly life and propose an earthly life that is not only anticipatory but also a

prefiguration of what is to come. The present day placement of the well at the garden's center recalls the rich symbolism of the historic cloister garden.

Eventually the Episcopal Diocese of South Florida acquired the former tourist attraction and the monastery became home to a living parish. The cloister, its refectory, and garden, serve the parish and the wider community. Their presence is a reminder of the *claritas* of Cistercian life, something that is directly and fully recalled in the architecture and discerned in the potential of the cloister garden.

–JL

Drawing class students at entrance loggia.
University of Miami School of Architecture.

Notes:

1. Larry Birger, "Famous Expert Now Ready to Reassemble Monastery," *Miami Daily News*, December 21, 1952.

2. "Press Release—Old Spanish Monastery," collection "Old Spanish Monastery Files."

3. Arthur Byne to William Randolph Hearst, October 10, 1926, Monastery Cloister, 20-21, Florida Collection, Miami-Dade Public Library.

4. Wolfgang Braunfels, *Monasteries of Western Europe: The Architecture of the Orders* (Princeton: Princeton University Press, 1972), 81.

5. Braunfels, 1972, 98.

6. Paul Meyvaert, "The Medieval Monastic Garden," in *Medieval Gardens*, (Washington D.C.: Dumbarton Oaks, 1986), 45.0.

7. Meyvaert, 1986, 49.

Drawing by: Julian Gonzalez, Stephen Hafer, Ahmad Khaldoon

36" x 36", square format, ink on mylar, 1994

Woodland view.
Photograph by R. Ceo.

Born in Orlando in 1884, Harry P. Leu's industrious nature and capable mind would, in a short period of time, propel him north to further his business education. In 1904 Harry Leu went to New York to study bookkeeping, shorthand, marketing, and sales management techniques. This education would serve him well when he was asked to return to Orlando to care for his family. Harry Leu's father had just passed away, and given that his sisters had moved away, Harry needed to care for his mother who had recently become ill. Although reluctant to leave behind the opportunities afforded him in the north, Harry Leu would eventually return to the Cain & O'Berry Boiler Company in Orlando where he had worked before going to New York to study. Working primarily as a "trouble-shooter" analyzing problems and writing orders for equipment and repairs, Harry Leu excelled, and

by 1925 he became a primary stockholder in the company. Harry Leu Inc. was eventually formed from the original company with a focus on the supply of industrial parts as opposed to their maintenance and repair.

By 1936 Harry P. Leu, and his new bride Mary Jane, visited a property that had previously caught his eye. Within the year he purchased the land. He soon made it his year-round residence and began to renovate the house extensively making major additions to the garden. These additions would later make the garden a drive-through attraction for Florida tourists. While the gardens he developed are now open to the public and owe their existence to the vision and boosterism of this man whose name is attached to them, the property and, most of all, the house upon it are products of a series of owners who had enhanced and enlarged the facilities since the 1870s. Working always with a sense of the importance of building upon the endeavors of earlier inhabitants, they left in the house and on the site a record of the development of Central Florida in general and of Orlando in particular.

Pioneer occupation here goes back to the late 1850s when the Mizell family homesteaded the land during the Seminole War. The new town that would become Orlando was then called Jernigan, after Aaron Jernigan who had established the first post office there in 1850. The land was full of pine woods, punctuated by pristine lakes and open grass prairies that made ideal pastures for cattle and later were planted with citrus and cotton. In 1857, Jernigan became Orlando and began to prosper on the profits of the citrus industry. By 1908, Orlando was calling itself "The City Beautiful" in recognition of extensive plantings of oak trees on its public land. Its population figures then rivaled those of St. Augustine and Miami. Even after a killing frost in 1894, the area, although devastated, continued to attract wealthy people from the northeast.

Landing view to rose garden.
Photograph by R. Ceo.

Leu House.
Photograph by R. Ceo.

One of them was Duncan C. Pell, from a socially prominent New York and Newport, Rhode Island family. Fresh from a difficult divorce, Pell bought the property from the Mizells in 1902. Shortly he took a soon-to-be-famous young star, Helen Louise Gardner, as his wife. They expanded the original house (which was a simple two-story wood frame structure) by adding a library and master bedroom wing; a formal dining room to the back with indoor plumbing; and a detached kitchen to keep the heat and cooking aromas away from the main house. The house transformed from a vernacular homestead into the comfortable country home of a well-to-do family more interested in polo than gardening.

The Pells also acquired the Mizell family cemetery with the property, and although they made improvements to the property, they preserved the small family cemetery and continued to maintain it.

In 1906 Joseph Hersey Woodward and his wife, Martha Burt Metcalf Woodward, acquired the house with a land parcel of forty acres. Joseph Woodward was a traveling salesman for his father's business, the La Belle Iron Works of Wheeling West Virginia. Economic setbacks in the late 1920s caused them to vacate the house and the site. Eventually the property was rented out, and fell into disrepair until Harry P. Leu and his new wife arrived in 1936. Mary Jane Leu recalls her first visit:

The house was standing in the midst of a heavy forest grove. The main estate drive came in from Nebraska (Avenue) through a pair of ornamental iron gates. The drive approached the lakeshore, turned toward the house and ended in a garage in back of the home. The road track continued west from the garage and connected with the main drive where the flower circle is today. A small cottage sat north of the road. It was used to house the grove foreman. Another small frame cottage was on the shore of Lake Rowena where a Valencia orange grove was planted.[1]

Her description of a site well traversed with roads giving access to the buildings and the grove suggests that the presence of roads would have a significant impact on the way Leu perceived the possibilities for developing a garden that would become public in 1961.

After purchasing the house with sixty acres of land in 1936, Harry Leu set to work improving it.

The land was full of pine woods, punctuated by pristine lakes and open grass prairies that made ideal pastures for cattle and later were planted with citrus and cotton.

The Leus traveled more than 30,000 miles throughout the Far East and southern Europe and collected specimens for their grounds.[2]

Rose garden.
Photograph by R. Ceo.

When they eventually deeded the garden to the city in 1961 they had planted more than 1,536 camellias and hundreds of azaleas, and their grounds also included groves and areas of native vegetation.

In addition to beautifying his own estate, Harry Leu became an active booster for Orlando and was instrumental in developing its road and highway system. His interest in roads may also have sparked his idea of making the property a drive-through garden. He opened it to motoring visitors in 1961 and, until 1970, they could drive through and view the gardens from their automobiles, a novel idea that was also tried out in 1936 at other tourist attractions in Florida, most notably the Ravine Gardens in Palatka. The drive-through experience would eventually become a staple for many gardens built as tourist attractions.

After the Leus' garden was deeded over to the city, the landscape architect Thomas H. Wallis Jr., was engaged to create its master plan. He modeled the design on the Golden Gate Park in San Francisco, suggesting that the dense native landscape should eventually give way to ten new, smaller gardens, each with a different theme and plant material. In his plan, an enlarged rose

Garden lawn.
Photograph by R. Ceo.

garden appeared, as well as a ravine garden, a white garden, a greenhouse, a floral clock, a conservatory, and a palm garden. The south and north woods would supply the necessary canopy of live oaks for the camellias and azaleas the most important collection on the grounds.

The Wallis plan was largely realized during the late 1960s and early 1970s due to contributions from the City of Orlando. The established model of the small themed garden in 1986 and the Wyckoff overlook and native wetland garden in 1989 added to the overall thematic structure of the garden. Most of these additions were made

possible by the generous donations of clubs and individuals.

The 1990s saw the continued growth of the garden. It was a period during which both staff and funds were added for continued success. Currently the Harry P. Leu Gardens encompass fifty-six acres within which the multi-layered process of its evolution from a private enterprise to a civic jewel is represented. This has been an exemplary achievement of the cumulative, collective effort of generations of preservationists.

–RJC

Notes:

1. Julie Cole, *Orlando's Leu House* (Friends of Harry P. Leu Gardens, Inc., 1995), 65.

2. Cole, 1995, 69.

LOCATIONS & CONTACTS

The Barnacle
3485 Main Highway
Coconut Grove, FL 33133-0995
(305) 448-9445

Bonnet House
900 North Birch Road
Fort Lauderdale, FL 33304-3326
(954) 563-5393

Charles Deering Estate
Deering Estate at Cutler
16701 Southwest 72nd Avenue
Miami, FL 33157-2500
(305) 235-1668

Cà d'Zan
5401 Bay Shore Road
Sarasota, FL 34243-2161
(941) 351-1660

Coral Castle
28655 South Dixie Highway
Homestead, FL 33033-1214
(305) 248-6345

Cluett Memorial Garden
Episcopal Church of Bethesda-
  by-the-Sea
141 South County Road
Palm Beach, FL 33480-6107
(561) 655-4554

Cypress Gardens
2641 South Lake Summit Drive
P.O. Box 1
Winter Haven, FL 33884-0001
(800) 282-2123

"Doc" Thomas House
Tropical Audubon Society
5530 Sunset Drive
Miami, FL 33143-5697
(305) 666-5111

Thomas A. Edison Estate & Gardens
2350 McGregor Boulevard
Fort Myers, FL 33901-3315
(941) 334-3614

El Jardin
Carrollton School of the Sacred Heart
3747 Main Highway
Coconut Grove, Florida 33133-5907
(305) 446-5673

Everglades City
Museum of the Everglades
105 West Broadway
P.O. Box 8
Everglades, FL 34139-0008
(941) 695-0008

Fairchild Tropical Garden
10901 Old Cutler Road
Coral Gables, Florida 33156-4296
(305) 667-1651

Four Arts Garden
2 Four Arts Plaza
Palm Beach, FL 33480-4102
(561) 655-7226

Greynolds Park
17530 West Dixie Highway
North Miami, FL 33160-4819
(305) 949-1741

Harry P. Leu Garden
1920 North Forest Avenue
Orlando, FL 32803-1537
(407) 246-2620

Henry Ford Winter Residence
2350 McGregor Boulevard
Fort Myers, FL 33901-3315
(941) 334-3614

Indian Key
P.O. Box 1052
(Florida Keys, Mile Marker 78.5)
Islamorada, FL 33036-1052
(305) 664-2540

The Kampong
4013 South Douglas Road
Coconut Grove, Florida 33133-6840
(305) 442-7169

Koreshan Unity Settlement
(US 41 at Corkscrew Road)
P.O. Box 7
Estero, FL 33928-0007
(941) 992-0311

Lignumvitae Key
(Offshore from Indian Key Fill
  in Florida Bay Mile Marker 78.5)
P.O. Box 1052
Islamorada, FL 33036-1052
(305) 664-2540

Matheson Hammock
9610 Old Cutler Road
Coral Gables, FL 33156-4268
(305) 665-5475

McKee Jungle Gardens
(Now McKee Botanical Garden)
350 U.S. Highway 1
Vero Beach, FL 32962-2906
(561) 794-0601

Mountain Lake Sanctuary
(Now Bok Tower Gardens)
1151 Tower Boulevard
Lake Wales, FL 33853-3412
(863) 676-1408

Parrot Jungle
11000 Southwest 57th Avenue
Miami, FL 33156-4199
(305) 666-7834

Ravine Gardens
1600 Twigg Street
P.O. Box 1096
Palatka, FL 32178-1096
(904) 329-3721

St. Bernard de Clairvaux
16711 West Dixie Highway
North Miami Beach, FL 33160-3714
(305) 945-1461

Vizcaya
3251 South Miami Avenue
Miami, FL 33129-2897
(305) 250-9133

BIBLIOGRAPHY

Neil Baldwin.
  Edison: Inventing the Century. New York: Hyperion, 1995.

A.D. Barnes.
  "History of Dade County Park System 1929-1969, The First Forty Years" 1986.
  File 5-23, William Lyman Phillips Papers, Research Center, Historical Museum of
  Southern Florida, Miami, Florida.

Jeanne Bellamy selected and edited.
  "The Perrines At Indian Key, 1838-1840." From: "Incidents in the Life of
  Hester Perrine Walker", a daughter of Dr. Henry Perrine, dated January 28, 1885.
  Tequesta, The Journal of The Historical Association of Southern Florida. No. 7 (1947).

Larry Birger.
  "Famous Expert Now Ready to Reassemble Monastery." *Miami Daily News*,
  December 21, 1952.

Edward W. Bok.
  "A Personal Foreword," in *The Sanctuary and Singing Tower*. Mountain Lake, Florida:
  The American Foundation Incorporated, 1929.

  Letter to Frederick Law Olmsted, Jr. 10 July 1922. File 7-22, William Lyman Phillips
  Papers, Research Center, Historical Museum of Southern Florida, Miami, Florida.

Wolfgang Braunfels.
  Monasteries of Western Europe: The Architecture of the Orders. Princeton: Princeton
  University Press, 1972.

Eleanor Bisbee.
  "It is Extremely Simple to Plant Cactus and the Deering Plantation Gives Proof that
  Western Varieties Will Grow Here." *The Miami Daily Metropolis*, Monday, September
  25, 1922.

Arthur Byne.
  Letter to William Randolph Hearst, October 10, 1926. Monastery Cloister, 20-21,
  Florida Collection, Miami-Dade Public Library.

Frank Button.
  "The Suburb Beautiful." *Coral Gables, Miami's Master Suburb*. 1921.

Susan Clark assisted by Sonia Blake, edited by John M. Delzell.
  A Historic Tour Guide of Palatka and Putnam County, Florida. Palatka, Florida:
  Putnam County Historical Society and Glanzer Press, 1992.

David Coffin.
  The Villa in the Life of Renaissance Rome. Princeton: Princeton University Press, (1979)
  1988.

Charles Deering.
  Letter to John Kunkel Small, May 31, 1925. Florida State Archive, in Janet Snyder
  Matthews, *Historical Documentation: The Charles Deering Estate at Cutler*, May 1992.

Marjory Stoneman Douglas.
  Dedication of the Fairchild Tropical Garden 22 March 1938. Miami: Fairchild Tropical
  Garden, 1938.

  The Everglades: River of Grass. Sarasota: Pineapple Press, (1947) 1988.

Andrew Jackson Downing.
  A Treatise on the Theory and Practice of Landscape Gardening. New York: A.O. Moore & Co.,
  (1841) 1859.

Beth Dunlop.
  "Inventing Antiquity: The Art and Craft of Mediterranean Revival Architecture," *Florida
  Theme Issue: The Journal of the Decorative and Propaganda Arts 1875-1945*, 23 (1998): 190-207.

Charles W. Eliot.
  Charles Eliot, Landscape Architect. Boston and New York: Houghton and Mifflin
  Company, 1902.

Pamela Euston.
  "'Big Boss' The Life and Times of Hugh Taylor Birch," unpublished paper for
  Dr. Paul S. George, Florida Atlantic University, April 24, 1989.

David Fairchild.
  The World Was My Garden. Reprint, Miami: Banyan Books Inc., for Fairchild Tropical
  Garden, (1938) 1982.

  The World Grows Round My Door. New York and London: Charles Scribner's Sons, 1947.

Henry Ford in collaboration with Samuel Crowther.
  My Life and Work. New York: Garden City Publishing Co., Inc., 1922.

Florence Fritz.
  Unknown Florida. Coral Gables: University of Miami Press, 1963.

Cory Gittner.
  Miami's Parrot Jungle and Gardens: The Colorful History of an Uncommon Attraction.
  Gainesville: University Press of Florida, 2000.

Kathryn Hall.
  The Pictorial History of The Episcopal Church of Bethesda-By-The-Sea, Palm Beach Florida.
  Published by the author (1970) 1986.

Kathryn Chapman Harwood.
  The Lives of Vizcaya. Miami: Banyan Press, 1985.

Franklin Hamilton Hazlehurst.
  Jacques Boyceau and the French Formal Garden. Athens: University of Georgia Press, 1966.

G.M. Herbert and I.S.K. Reeves.
  "Koreshan Unity Settlement 1894 – 1977." Restoration Study for the Department of
  Natural Resources. Division of Recreation and Parks, State of Florida, 1977.

Cathy Hollopeter and Bonita Banner.
  "Koreshan Solar Festival Commemorates Founder's Birth." *The American Eagle*. Vol. 66
  No. 195 (June 1985).

Faith Reyher Jackson.
  Pioneer of Tropical Landscape Architecture: William Lyman Phillips in Florida. Gainesville:
  University of Florida Press, 1997.

Mrs. Alfred G. Kay.
  "History of the Four Arts Garden," *The Four Arts Garden: History and Catalogue of
  Important Specimens*. Palm Beach: The Garden Club of Palm Beach, 1978.

Dorothy C. Kelly.
  "Jungles and Junkets," *House and Garden* (December 1940): 41.

Koresh [Cyrus R. Teed].
  The Cellular Cosmogony: The Earth a Concave Sphere. 1898. reprint. Estero: The Koreshan
  Unity, (1922) 1983.

Koreshan Unity Co-Operative.
  The Solution of Industrial Problems. Estero: The Guiding Star Publishing House, 1907.

Edward Leedskalnin.
    A Book In Every Home. Published by the author, Homestead, Florida, 1936.

Stefan Lorant, editor.
    The New World: The First Pictures of America made by John White and Jacques le Moyne and engraved by Theodore de Bry with Contemporary Narratives of the Huguenot Settlement in Florida 1562-65 and the Virgina Colony 1585-1590. New York: Duell, Sloan & Pearce, 1946.

Joseph Lloyd.
    "Koreshan Unity Plant Nursery and Botanical Gardens." *The American Eagle* Vol. 68, No. 199 (April 1987): 8.

Catherine Lynn.
    "Dream and Substance: Araby and the Planning of Opa-locka," *Florida Theme Issue: The Journal of the Decorative and Propaganda Arts 1875-1945.* 23 (1998): 163-189.

Elliot J. Mackle, Jr.
    "The Koreshan Unity in Florida 1894-1910." Master's Thesis, University of Miami, 1971.

James T. Maher.
    The Twilight of Splendor. Boston and Toronto: Little, Brown and Company, 1975.

Janet Snyder Matthews.
    Historical Documentation: The Charles Deering Estate at Cutler. Metro Dade County Park and Recreation Department, May 1992.

Michael McDonough.
    "Selling Sarasota: Architecture and Propaganda in a 1920s BoomTown." *Florida Theme Issue: The Journal of the Decorative and Propaganda Arts 1875-1945.* 23 (1998): 11-31.

Paul Meyvaert.
    "The Medieval Monastic Garden," in *Medieval Gardens.* Elisabeth B. MacDougall, editor. Washington D.C.: Dumbarton Oaks, 1986, 25-53.

Brian E. Michaels.
    The River Flows North: A History of Putnam County, Florida. Texas: Taylor Publishing Company, (1976) 1986.

Olivia Gazzam Morrish.
    A History of The Society of the Four Arts, Palm Beach, Florida: A Narrative of Significant Events from 1936 to 1983.

Kirk Munroe.
    Big Cypress: The Story of An Everglade Homestead. Boston: W.A. Wilde & Co., 1894.

Ralph Middleton Munroe and Vincent Gilpin.
    The Commodore's Story. New York: Washburn, 1930. Reprint. Historical Association of Southern Florida, 1990.

Dr. Henry Nehrling.
    My Garden In Florida and Miscellaneous Horticultural Notes. Vol. I. From a collection of manuscripts originally published by *The American Eagle.* Estero, Florida: Koreshan Unity Press, 1944.

Allan Nevins and Frank Ernest Hill.
    Ford: Expansion and Challenge 1915-1933. New York: Charles Scribner's Sons, 1957.

No author cited:

    "An Artist of the Out-of-Doors Made Coral Gables a City of Beauty Spots." *The Herald,* Miami, Florida, August 17, 1924.

    "Charles Deering Dies in Florida." *The New York Times,* Monday February 7, 1927, 19.

    "Crowds Put Seal of Approval upon 10th Flower Show: Exhibit This Year Is Smaller But Staged With Unusual Merit." *Palm Beach Post,* Saturday Morning, February 26, 1938.

    Flaming Sword. Volume 9, No.10 (1895): 204.

    Flaming Sword. Volume 10, No. 10 (October 1896): 226.

    Flaming Sword. (April 17, 1906): 6.

    "Four Arts Society has Gained Prominent Place in Resort Program; Opens Dec.1." *The Palm Beach Times,* November 20, 1938.

    "Garden Club Views Reconstruction Work in Four Arts Society Gardens." *Palm Beach Post,* Thursday, March 25, 1948.

    Genesis 1:11-31

    http://weather.unisys.com/hurricane/atlantic/1947/index.html

    "Koreshan Unity Alliance Members to Lobby State Legislators for Founder's House," and "The Koreshan Unity Alliance Seeks New Members." *The American Eagle.* Vol.74 No. 205 (April 1990): 3.

    A Monograph of the Florida Work of Kiehnel & Elliott Architects. Miami, 1938.

    Official Register of Harvard University. 6 (September 1909).

    "Press Release—Old Spanish Monastery," Collection "Old Spanish Monastery Files."

    Two New Gardens Planned For Show." *Palm Beach Post,* Friday Morning, February 17, 1939.

    "Vizcaya." *Harper's Bazaar.* (July 1917): 40-43.

    "Vizcaya, the Villa and Grounds." *The Architectural Review.* 5, no. 7 (July 1917):121-140.

    "Work On the Four Arts Building Begun." *Palm Beach Sun,* Friday July 25, 1947.

    "Mable and Edith are the best Known of the Ringlings." *St. Petersburg Times,* January 30, 1966, 4.

Frederick Law Olmsted, Jr.
    Letter to Edward Bok. 7 July 1922. File 7-22, William Lyman Phillips Papers, Research Center, Historical Museum of Southern Florida, Miami, Florida.

    Letter to Edward Bok. 28 March 1931. File 7-22, William Lyman Phillips Papers, Research Center, Historical Museum of Southern Florida, Miami, Florida.

    Letter to William Lyman Phillips. 16 January 1935, File 7-5, William Lyman Phillips Papers, Research Center, Historical Museum of Southern Florida, Miami, Florida.

Frederick Law Olmsted, Sr.
    Forty Years of Landscape Architecture: Central Park, eds. Frederick Law Olmsted, Jr. and Theodora Kimball. Cambridge, Massachusetts and London England: The M.I.T. Press, (1928) 1973.

John Onians.
    Bearers of Meaning: The Classical Orders in Antiquity, the Middle Ages, and the Renaissance. Princeton: Princeton University Press, 1989.

Phineas Paist.
    Letter to Charles Deering. July 10, 1922. Box 4, Charles Deering Photo prints, Research Center, Historical Museum of Southern Florida, Miami, Florida.

Arva Moore Parks and Gregory W. Bush, with Laura Pincus.
    Miami The American Crossroad A Centennial Journey 1896-1990. Needham Heights, MA: Simon & Schuster Custom Publishing, 1996.

William Patterson.
    "A Florida Echo of the Glory of Old Venice." *Town & Country* (July 20, 1917): 23-30.

Henry Perrine.
    Letter to the Committee on Agriculture, House, U.S. Congress. February 3, 1838. Library of The Gray Herbarium Archives, Harvard University.

William Lyman Phillips.
    Class notes by William Lyman Phillips. 1908. File 23-5, William Lyman Phillips Papers, Research Center, Historical Museum of Southern Florida, Miami, Florida.

Letter to Frank Albert Waugh. 30 October 1915. File 14-5, William Lyman Phillips Papers, Research Center, Historical Museum of Southern Florida.

Letter to Waldo E. Sexton. Lake Wales, June 4, 1931, 1, Research Center, Historical Museum of Southern Florida.

Letter to Waldo E. Sexton. Lake Wales, Oct 13, 1931. Research Center, Historical Museum of Southern Florida.

Report to National Park Service, "Narrative Report, Months of January 1935 and February 1935." RG 79, Florida SP-2. National Archives, College Park, Maryland.

Letter to Waldo E. Sexton. Miami, April 18, 1935. Research Center, Historical Museum of Southern Florida.

Report to National Park Service, "Narrative Report, Months of June and July 1935." RG-79, Florida SP-2, Box #15, National Archives, College Park, Maryland.

Report to National Park Service, Oct.-Nov. 1935. RG-79, Box 15. National Archives, College Park, Maryland.

Report to National Park Service, "Special Narrative Report, March 31, 1936." RG 79, Florida SP-2, Box #15, National Archives, College Park, Maryland.

Report to Karl Dahlberg. 27 July 1938, File 6-3. William Lyman Phillips Papers, Research Center, Historical Museum of Southern Florida, Miami, Florida.

Letter to Waldo E. Sexton. Miami, August 7, 1938. Research Center, Historical Museum of Southern Florida.

Letter to Colonel Robert Montgomery. 17 July 1941. File 13-11. William Lyman Phillips Papers, Research Center, Historical Museum of Southern Florida, Miami, Florida.

Letter to Colonel Robert Montgomery, 3 June 1942. File 13-11. William Lyman Phillips Papers, Research Center, Historical Museum of Southern Florida, Miami, Florida.

"The Mountain Lake Sanctuary, Mountain Lake, Florida: A Report." Olmsted Brothers, Landscape Architects, Brookline, Massachusetts and William Lyman Phillips, Landscape Architect, North Miami, Florida. 2 July 1956. File 8-4, William Lyman Phillips Papers, Research Center, Historical Museum of Southern Florida, Miami, Florida.

Letter to William Bell Marquis. 12 April 1958. Files 5-7, William Lyman Phillips Papers, Historical Museum of Southern Florida, Miami, Florida.

Letter to William Bell Marquis and Edward Clark Whiting 14 April 1958. File 5-7, William Lyman Phillips Papers, Research Center, Historical Museum of Southern Florida, Miami, Florida.

"The Fairchild Tropical Garden: A Memoir." 3 September 1958. File 13-14. William Lyman Phillips Papers, Research Center, Historical Museum of Southern Florida, Miami, Florida.

James Sturgis Pray.
"The Department of Landscape Architecture in Harvard University." *Landscape Architecture*, I, no. 2 (January 1911).

Winton H. Reinsmith.
Letter to William Lyman Phillips. Vero Beach, July 23, 1930. Research Center, Historical Museum of Southern Florida, Miami, Florida.

Letter to William Lyman Phillips. Vero Beach, August 12, 1931. Research Center, Historical Museum of Southern Florida, Miami, Florida.

Letter to William Lyman Phillips. Vero Beach, August 23, 1931. Research Center, Historical Museum of Southern Florida, Miami, Florida.

Jayne Rice.
Reflections of a Legacy: The Bonnet House Story. Fort Lauderdale: Bonnet House, 1989.

Ivan Rodriguez and Margot Ammidown.
From Wilderness to Metropolis: The History and Architecture of Dade County, Florida 1825-1940. Miami: Metropolitan Dade County, 1982.

Lee Rogers.
"Palm Beach Flower Show is a Veritable Realm of Beauty," *Palm Beach Daily News*, Saturday, February 26, 1938.

O.C. Simonds.
Landscape Gardening. (New York: The Macmillan Company, 1920) reprint edition, Amherst: University of Massachusetts Press in association with the Library of American Landscape History, 2000.

Charles Torrey Simpson.
Ornamental Gardening in Florida. Little River, Florida, 1916.

John Kunkel Small.
From Eden to Sahara: Florida's Tragedy. Lancaster, PA: The Science Press Printing Company, 1929.

Photographs, J.K. Small Collection, Florida Department of State, Division of Library and Information Services, Bureau of Archives and Records Management, online at: http://www.dos.state.fl.us/fpc

Memo to J. N. Morrison, undated, "Planting at Cutler, Note number 100. Folder 5, Research Center, Historical Museum of Southern Florida, Miami, Florida.

Michael Snodin and Elisabet Stavenow-Hidemark, editors.
Carl and Karin Larsson: Creators of the Swedish Style. New York: Bulfinch Press, (1997) 1998.

Diego Suarez.
Untitled recollection on the design of the gardens. 1953. Vizcaya Archive.

Charlton Tebeau.
Florida's Last Frontier: The History of Collier County. Coral Gables, Florida: University of Miami Press, (1957) 1966.

Maria Turney.
"Koreshan Unity Settlement," http://getp.freac.fsu.edu/fga/places/koreshan.htm

Ellen J. Uguccioni.
"Report of the City of Coral Gables Planning Department Historic Preservation Division to the Historic Preservation Board on the Designation of Matheson Hammock Park as an Historic District." March 1992.

Richard K. Webel.
"Gardens to Visit: Tropical Plantings in Palm Beach Inspire Artists and Hobbyists." *The New York Times*, February 22, 1959.

Gerard Wertkin.
"Solar Festival Celebrates 145th Anniversary." *The American Eagle* Vol. 65 No. 194 (October 1984): 1.

Thomas Whately.
Observations on Modern Gardening, Illustrated by Descriptions. 3rd Ed. London: T. Payne, 1771.

Bertram Zuckerman.
The Kampong: The Fairchild's Tropical Paradise. Miami: National Tropical Botanical Garden and Fairchild Tropical Garden, 1993.

INDEX

ABOUT THE AUTHORS

Rocco Ceo is an Associate Professor at the University of Miami School of Architecture.
He has produced drawings of the elements of Florida's landscapes as well as a documentation of the Marjory Stoneman Douglas home.
His published work includes the award winning study, *Redland: A Preservation and Tourism Plan*, done with
Margot Ammidown and Maria Nardi. He practices architecture and has most recently completed the restoration of the
Paul C. Ransom cottage at Ransom Everglades school in Coconut Grove.

Joanna Lombard is a Professor at the University of Miami School of Architecture.
She has written a chapter on the landscape of Coral Gables in *Coral Gables An American Garden City*,
and an essay on "The Memorable Landscapes of William Lyman Phillips," in the *Florida Theme Issue: The Journal of the
Decorative and Propaganda Arts*. With Denis Hector she practices architecture and is completing work on a garden
originally designed in 1945 by William Lyman Phillips.